3:16

The Numbers of Hope

WITH TEEN RESPONSES

ALSO BY MAX LUCADO

Every Day Deserves a Chance
Teen Edition

Facing Your Giants
Teen Edition adapted by Monica Hall

He Chose You
with story adaptations by Monica Hall

It's Not About Me
Teen Edition

Just Like Jesus
with teen story adaptations by Monica Hall

Next Door Savior
with teen story adaptations by Monica Hall

Published in Nashville, Tennessee, by Thomas Nelson. Thomas Nelson is a registered trademark of Thomas Nelson, Inc.

Thomas Nelson, Inc., books may be purchased in bulk for educational, business, fund-raising, or sales promotional use. For information, please e-mail SpecialMarkets@ThomasNelson.com.

Karen Hill, Executive Editor for Max Lucado.

Interior art and page design by Casey Hooper

Library of Congress Cataloging-in-Publication Data

Lucado, Max.
  3:16 : the numbers of hope / by Max Lucado ; with teen responses by Tricia Goyer.
    p. cm.
  Includes bibliographical references (p.   ).
  ISBN 978-1-4003-1108-8 (pbk.)
  1. Bible. N.T. John III, 16—Criticism, interpretation, etc. 2. Salvation—Christianity.
  3. God—Love. 4. Teenagers—Religious life. I. Goyer, Tricia. II. Title.
  BS2615.6.S25L83 2007b
  226.5'06—dc22   2007032728

Printed in the United States of America

10 11 12 13 14 RRD 12 11 10 9 8

Mfg. RRD / Crawfordsville, IN / April 2010 / PO # 107484

3:16®

The Numbers of Hope

Max Lucado

Teen Responses by
Tricia Goyer

THOMAS NELSON
Since 1798

NASHVILLE DALLAS MEXICO CITY RIO DE JANEIRO

With pride as deep and powerful as the Gulf Stream,
Denalyn and I dedicate this book
to our daughter Sara on her eighteenth birthday.
If you receive half the joy you've given us,
you'll radiate the rest of your life.
We love you.

contents

Contents

acknowledgments

A word to some special folks who brought this book to life:

Tricia Goyer—thanks for lending your voice and that of your outstanding teen team to this edition.

Beverly Phillips and June Ford—your editorial skills are unmatched!

Patti Evans and Casey Hooper—look in the dictionary under 'creative design' and you'll find your names.

And especially to the Giver of all words: Eternal thanks, dear King. Would you convince the ones who read these words that the best of life is yet to be?

introduction

What do teens think of John 3:16? That was the question put to me. In my search to know the answer, I asked guys and girls from throughout the country to tell me their fears and struggles, their hopes and dreams. I discovered many of their thoughts were similar. And many had unique observations that caused me to laugh out loud. Overall, their comments showed the wonderful humor and wisdom of teens as they relate to life and truth.

I combined the numerous comments of all the teens I interviewed into the thoughts of two fictional characters, Justin and Becca.

Justin is sixteen. His parents are divorced and thoughts of God are new to him. He likes to play the guitar and hang out with friends. He also likes video games, basketball, and surfing the Internet. Justin is trying to follow God, but he has many ups and downs. He's thankful, though, that he doesn't have to depend on his strength alone. You will notice Justin's faith growing through these pages

as he connects with God and discovers the ultimate love found in 3:16.

$Becca$ is seventeen. She was raised attending
church. The harder struggle for Becca is applying
what she learns on Sunday to real life. Becca is
thankful that she grew up knowing about God, but
she also realizes that she's just beginning to apply
what she's learned to how she lives. Becca has
some of the same struggles as most teen girls: con-
flict with her parents, bad decisions in the past concerning guys, a weak self-image, and struggles in not
treating others as lovingly as she should. Yet Becca
has a heart that longs to do what is right, and she
turns to God often to help her in her daily life.

I hope you enjoy connecting with the thoughts of
Justin and Becca through the pages of this book. Some
of their confessions might be yours. Some of their prayers
too. Feel free to pray along with them, or change their
words to your own. As both Justin and Becca (and the
teens they represent) have learned, God is always longing
to listen, whether you turn to him for help and guidance
. . . or you just want to offer a little praise to him. He's
always available with arms wide open in loving welcome.

And I give a special thank you to the teens who contributed to the prayers, praise, confessions, and struggles of Justin and Becca:

Lauren Clark

Grant Gonzalez

Cory Goyer

Leslie Goyer

Anna Hawkins

Loundy Hilton

Grayson Leder

David Losie

Shane Madden

Jason McDonald

Bobby Nordlund

Dallas Rayburn

Hannah Sowell

Cole Warren

Sarah Warren

Matthew Welborn

Maheem Welcome

1

What will my friends think?

He's waiting for the shadows. Darkness will provide the cover he wants. So he waits for the safety of nightfall. He sits near the second-floor window of his house, watching the sunset, waiting for the right time. Waiting.

Tonight Nicodemus goes where no one who knows him would believe. Tomorrow morning he'll go where everyone expects him to be. He will gather with religious leaders like he does every morning and do what religious leaders do: discuss God. Discuss reaching God, pleasing God, appeasing God. God.

Pharisees talk about God. And Nicodemus sits among them. Debating. Pondering. Solving puzzles about God.

What does God say? Nicodemus needs to know. It's his job. He's a holy man and leads holy men. His name appears on the elite list of Torah scholars. He dedicated his life to the law and occupies one of the seventy-one seats of the Judean supreme court. He has credentials, clout, and questions.

Justin, 16

Like Nicodemus, I have lots of questions I'd like to ask God. For starters:
- Who are you?
- Who am I?
- Why was I born now and into *this* family?
- Why did you go to the trouble to create such a beautiful world?
- Why is there a hell?
- Why do you love me no matter what I do?

And as long as I'm asking, would you mind telling me: What is the purpose of snakes, mosquitoes, and fleas? *

Questions for this Galilean preacher. The man who has ample time for the down-and-out crowd but little time for religious leaders.

* Write your own thoughts and questions in the *My Notes* section starting on page 157.

So Nicodemus comes at night. His friends can't know of the meeting. They wouldn't understand. As the shadows darken the city, Nicodemus steps out, slips unseen through the winding streets. He passes servants lighting lamps in the courtyards and takes a path that ends at the door of a simple house. Jesus and his followers are staying here, he's been told. Nicodemus knocks.

The noisy room silences as Nicodemus enters. The men are wharf workers and tax collectors, unaccustomed to the highbrow world of a scholar. They squirm in their seats. Silence.

Justin, 16

I understand how Nicodemus felt. I want to know Jesus better too. Sometimes I feel like I'm the only one. It's not that my friends hate God or anything. They just don't seem to care. Nicodemus came to you at night, when he didn't have to face anyone else. Here it is. Night. I'm alone.

Thinking. Praying. Asking questions.

Wondering who you are and why you made me. Wondering what it takes to know you better. Wondering what you want from me.

The awkward silence ends as Nicodemus begins the most famous conversation in the Bible: "Rabbi, we know that You are a teacher come from God; for no one can do these signs that You do unless God is with him" (John 3:2 NKJV).

Nicodemus begins with what he "knows." *I've done my homework,* he implies. *Your work impresses me.*

We wait for Jesus to return the compliment. "And I've heard of you, Nicodemus."

> YOUR BEST WON'T DO. YOUR WORKS DON'T WORK. YOUR FINEST EFFORTS DON'T mean squat. UNLESS YOU ARE BORN AGAIN, YOU can't even see WHAT GOD IS UP TO.

None comes. Jesus makes no mention of Nicodemus's VIP status or good intentions, not because they don't exist, but because, according to Jesus, they just don't matter. He simply issues this proclamation: "Unless one is born again, he cannot see the kingdom of God" (3:3 NKJV).

Behold the Continental Divide of Scripture, the International Date Line of faith. Nicodemus stands on one side, Jesus on the other, and Christ pulls no punches about their differences.

Nicodemus lives in a land of good efforts, sincere

gestures, and hard work. Give God your best and God does the rest.

Jesus's response? Your best won't do. Your works don't work. Your finest efforts don't mean squat. Unless you are born again, you can't even see what God is up to.

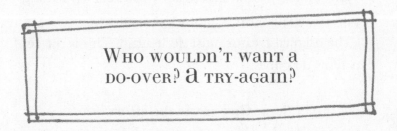

WHO WOULDN'T WANT A DO-OVER? A TRY-AGAIN?

Nicodemus hesitates. Born again? "How can a man be born when he is old?" (3:4 NKJV). You must be kidding. Put life in reverse? Rewind the tape? Start all over? We can't be born again.

Oh, but wouldn't we like to? A do-over. A try-again.

Jesus doesn't crack a smile. "Most assuredly, I say to you, unless one is born of water and the Spirit, he cannot enter the kingdom of God" (3:5 NKJV). About this time a gust of wind blows a few leaves through the still-open door. Jesus picks one off the floor and holds it up. God's power works like that wind, Jesus explains. Newborn hearts are born of heaven. You can't wish, earn, or create one. New birth? Inconceivable. God handles the task, start to finish.

Nicodemus looks around the room at the followers. Their blank expressions betray equal bewilderment.

Born again. Birth, by definition, is a passive act. The child contributes nothing to the delivery. Mom deserves the gold. She exerts the effort. She pushes, agonizes, and delivers.

The mother pays the price of birth. The baby doesn't do any of the work. Likewise, a spiritual rebirthing requires a capable parent, not an able infant.

The original creator must do it again. This is the act that Jesus describes.

Born: God exerts the effort.
Again: God restores the beauty.

We don't *try* again. We need not the muscle of self but a miracle of God. The thought strikes Nicodemus as insane. "How can this be?" (3:9). Jesus answers by leading him to the Hope diamond of the Bible.

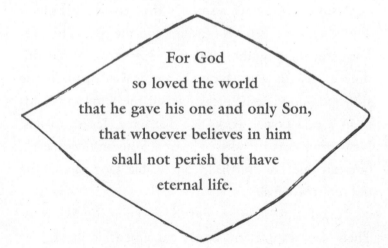

**For God
so loved the world
that he gave his one and only Son,
that whoever believes in him
shall not perish but have
eternal life.**

A twenty-six-word parade of hope: beginning with God, ending with life, and urging us to do the same. Brief enough to write on a napkin or memorize in a moment, yet solid enough to weather two thousand years of storms and questions. If you know nothing of the Bible, start here. If you know everything in the Bible, return here. We all need the reminder.

Becca, 17

Once I got to pick a plastic toy ring out of a "treasure chest" because I had memorized a Bible verse. I was, like, five or something. I lost that ring by the next morning . . . but I still remember the words of the verse by heart. It was John 3:16.

Now I get why kids learn this verse first. It shows what love is all about. Not flowers, chocolate, and the sappy kiss at the end of movies—although I like those sometimes too! But real love that gave everything, gave his Son. It is a laser pointing to the very heart of God. More than any verse in the Bible, John 3:16 helps me understand who God is and what he has done for me.

The heart of the human problem is the heart of the human. And God's treatment is prescribed in John 3:16.

He loves.
He gave.
We believe.
We live.

The words are to Scripture what the Mississippi River is to America—an entryway into the heartland. Believe or dismiss them, embrace or reject them, any serious consideration of Christ must include them. Could you ponder the words of Christ and never understand John 3:16?

Read it again, slowly and aloud, and note the word that snatches your attention. "For God so loved the world that he gave his one and only Son, that whoever believes in him shall not perish but have eternal life."

"God so *loved* the world . . ." We'd expect an anger-fueled God. One who punishes the world, recycles the world, forsakes the world, . . . but loves the world?

The *world*? This world? With all the horrible things that go on—child abuse, hunger, poverty, war . . . ? And God loves the world so much he gave his:

Rules?

Dicta?

Edicts?

No. The heart-stilling, mind-bending, deal-making-or-breaking claim of John 3:16 is this: *God gave his son*

. . . *his only son.* Scripture equates Jesus with God. God, then, gave himself. Why? So that *"whoever* believes in him shall not perish."

Whoever . . . a universal word.

And *perish* . . . a sobering word. We'd like to dilute, if not delete, the term. Not Jesus. He pounds Do Not Enter signs on every square inch of Satan's gate and tells those hell-bent on entering to do so over his dead body. Even so, some souls insist.

In the end, some perish and some live. And what determines the difference? Not talents or what you do, not who you are or your possessions. Nicodemus had all of these. The difference is determined by our belief. "Whoever *believes* in him shall not perish but have eternal life."

Becca, 17

Nicodemus did what he thought was right. I mean, he was a religious leader. He did spend his days talking about God and reading scriptures. In comparison to the world, he must have been a really good person.

Sometimes it seems like my life is spent on trying to

make the world happy. My teachers, parents, friends . . . youth leaders. Compared to the world, face it, I am a really good person. Compared to most of the girls at my high school, I'd get the gold star. What is that goofy saying my dad would tell my brother and me: "Don't drink or smoke or chew and don't go with girls who do"? Well, I don't drink or smoke or cheat or lie (much). I gotta keep telling myself I'm missing the point, and I can never do or be good enough. . . . I mean, my good grades or perfect driving record or youth group car wash won't get me into heaven.

But I'd be lying if I said I spend tons of time thinking about meeting God's standards. It's easier to compare myself to others. Nobody's perfect, and some are far, far from it.

God, thank you that the "whoever" in that verse is me. My name. My life. Sin is sin. Dark hearts compared to dark hearts still separate me from you. That's where you come in, Jesus. Here you go. I'll take you up on that do-over.

THINK IT OVER

Have you ever hidden your search for God from friends?
If so, why?

_____

_____

_____

_____

For you, what's the hardest thing about God's character
to understand?

_____

_____

_____

_____

In what ways do you want to be like God?

_____

_____

_____

_____

Who is God?

3:16—"For *God* so loved the world . . ."

If only I could talk to the pilot. Thirty seconds would do. Face-to-face. Just so I could explain. He was, after all, the one bumping my wife and me from his plane.

Not that I could blame him. Denalyn had picked up more than souvenirs in Hong Kong. She was so nauseous I had to wheelchair her through the airport. She flopped onto her seat and pillowed her head against the window, and I promised to leave her alone for the fourteen-hour flight.

I had a simple goal: get Denalyn on the plane.

The airline staff had an opposite one: get Denalyn off.

Blame me for their fear. When a worried flight attendant asked about my wife's condition, I sent shock waves through the fuselage with my answer: "Virus." Attendants hurried to our seats like police at a crime scene.

"How long has she been sick?"

"Did you see a doctor?"

"Have you considered swimming home?"

I downplayed Denalyn's condition. "Give us one barf bag, and we're happy travelers." No one laughed. The news of a virus reached the pilot, and the pilot made a decision: "Not on my plane."

"You must leave," his bouncer informed us matter-of-factly.

"Says who?"

"The pilot."

> Can we assume THERE'S
> a PILOT BEHIND THE STEEL DOOR?

I leaned sideways and looked down the aisle for the man in charge, but the cockpit door was closed. *Coward.* I wanted to plead my case, but the man in charge was unavailable for comment. He had a 747 to fly, a seven-thousand-mile trip . . . and no time for us.

Can you relate? You may feel the same about the pilot of the universe. God: the too-busy-for-you commander in chief. Even worse, you may suspect a vacant captain's seat. How do we know a hand secures the controls? Can we assume there's a pilot behind the steel door?

Justin, 16

How can I be sure God's hand holds the controls to my life? I can't see him. Can't touch him. And that's the hard part.

When I was a little kid, I couldn't wait to grow up. There were tons of rules and too many people getting on my case. It seemed like being young was the worst punishment ever. But maybe it's the opposite. I've messed up enough to worry if one of these days I'm going to really blow it. There are times I could use someone bigger and wiser to help me out. Is God that someone?

Some days I can tell God is in charge just by the stuff that happens. But other times . . . well, to be honest I have to admit I have doubts. Doesn't everyone? Or is it just me that forgets to examine the evidence of God's existence?

This is where Christ comes in. He escorts passengers to the cockpit, enters 3:16 in the keypad, and unlocks the door to God. "For *God* so loved the world . . ."

Jesus assumes what Scripture declares: *God is.*

For proof, look up at the sky. That fuzzy band of white light is our galaxy, the Milky Way. One hundred billion stars.[1] Our galaxy is one of billions of others![2] Who can understand such a universe, let alone more universes than we could count?

No one can. But let's try anyway. Suppose you attempt to drive to the sun. A car dealer offers you a sweet deal on a space vehicle that averages 150 mph. You hop in, open the moon roof, and blast off. You drive nonstop, twenty-four hours a day, 365 days a year. Any guess as to the length of your trip? Try 70 years!

Suppose, after stretching your legs and catching a bit of sun, you fuel up and rocket off to Alpha Centauri, the next closest star system. Best pack a lunch and clear your calendar. You'll need 15 million years to make the trip.[3]

Don't like to drive, you say? Board a jet, and zip through our solar system at a blistering 600 mph. In 16.5 days you'll reach the moon, in 17 years you'll pass the sun, and in 690 years you can enjoy dinner on Pluto. After seven centuries you haven't even left our solar system, much less our galaxy.[4]

Our universe speaks of God. "The heavens declare the glory of God" (Psalm 19:1). A house implies a builder; a painting suggests a painter. Don't stars suggest a star maker? Look above you.

Now look within you. Look at your sense of right and wrong. Somehow even as a child you knew it was wrong to hurt people and right to help them. Who told you? Who says? Could your conscience have been from God?

You aren't alone. Every culture has frowned upon selfishness and celebrated courage. Even cannibals display rudimentary justice, usually refusing to eat their children.[5] A universal standard exists. Just as a code writer connects computers with common software bundles, a common

> ## COULD YOUR CONSCIENCE HAVE BEEN FROM GOD?

code connects people. We may violate or ignore the code, but we can't deny it. Even people who have never heard God's name sense his law within them. "There is something deep within [humanity] that echoes God's yes and no, right and wrong" (Romans 2:15 MSG). When atheists decry injustice, they can thank God for the ability to discern it. The conscience is God's fingerprint, proof of his existence.

Heavens above, moral code within. Someone got this plane airborne, and it wasn't any of us. There is a pilot, and he is unlike anyone we've seen.

"To whom, then, will you compare God?" the prophet asks (Isaiah 40:18). To whom indeed?

Hence, he always is. "Before the mountains were brought forth, or ever You had formed the earth and the world, even from everlasting to everlasting, You *are* God" (Psalm 90:2 NKJV).

God never began and will never cease. He exists endlessly, always. "The number of His years is unsearchable" (Job 36:26 NASB).

Even so, let's try to search them. Let every speck of sand, from the Sahara to South Beach, represent a billion years of God's existence. With some super vacuum, suck and then blow all the particles into a mountain, and count how many you have. Multiply your total by a billion and listen as God reminds: "They don't represent a fraction of my existence."

He is "the eternal God" (Romans 16:26). He invented time and owns the patent. "The day is yours, and yours also the night" (Psalm 74:16). He was something before anything else was. When the first angel lifted the first wing, God had already always been.

Most staggering of all, he has never messed up. Not once. The prophet Isaiah described his glimpse of God. He saw six-winged angels. Though sinless, they covered themselves in God's presence. Two wings covered eyes, two wings covered feet, and two carried the angels airborne. They volleyed one phrase back and forth: "Holy, holy, holy is the LORD of hosts" (Isaiah 6:3 NKJV).

> ### Becca, 17
>
> #### My Praise to God
>
> God, you are holy. You are so big I can't conceive and so close I can feel you in my heart. You created the entire world and you care about me. Sin cannot exist in your presence and yet you welcome me to your holy throne, because I believe in your son. With billions of people needing your attention, you hear my every thought. You knew me before I was born, and you know everywhere I go, every thought I think, every smile, every tear. You allow me in the glory of heaven where there are no tears, no sadness, no regrets. The vast universe is in your hands, and yet you are so tender with my small heart.

God is holy. Every decision, exact. Each word, appropriate. Never out-of-bounds or out of place. Not even tempted to make a mistake.

Tally this up. No needs. No age. No sin. No wonder he said, "I am God, and there is none like me" (Isaiah 46:9).

But is God's grandness good news? Smart pilots boot

sick people off the plane. An all-powerful God might do likewise.

In the cockpit: God, who has no needs, age, or sin. Bouncing in the back of the plane: Max. Burger dependent. Half-asleep. Compared to God, I have the life span of a fruit fly.

And sinless? I can't maintain a holy thought for two minutes. Should we fear God's greatness? We should if we didn't have the next four words of John 3:16: "For God *so loved the world.*"

> I can't maintain a HOLY
> THOUGHT FOR TWO minutes.

The one who formed you pulls for you. Untrumpable power stoked by unstoppable love. "If God is for us, who can be against us?" (Romans 8:31).

God does for you what Bill Tucker's father did for him. Bill was sixteen years old when his dad suffered a health crisis and had to leave his business. Even after Mr. Tucker regained his health, the Tucker family struggled financially, barely getting by.

Then Mr. Tucker came up with an idea. He won the bid to reupholster the chairs at the local movie theater. This stunned his family. He had never stitched a seat. He didn't even own a sewing machine. Still, he found someone to

QUIZ

Add up the points to see how you stand.

+ 5 POINTS: Read Bible today.

- 5 POINTS: Talked back to parents.

+10 POINTS: Prayed for enemies.

-10 POINTS: Went a whole day without even thinking about God.

+15 POINTS: Attended church . . . and youth group.

-15 POINTS: Slammed door on sibling's face.

+50 POINTS: Witnessed to a friend and he prayed to accept Jesus.

-50 POINTS: Driving too fast and . . . crash.

How did you do? *Not bad* . . . or *I'm in trouble?*
See what God thinks of that:

+30 to +80: God loves you completely.

+ 5 to +30: God loves you completely.

+ 5 to -80: God loves you completely.

teach him and located an industrial-strength machine. The family scraped together every cent they had to buy it. They drained savings accounts and dug coins out of the sofa. Finally, they had enough.

It was a fine day when Bill rode with his dad to pick up the equipment. Bill remembers a jovial, hour-long trip talking about their bright future. They loaded the machine in the back of their truck and secured it right behind the cab. Mr. Tucker then invited his son to drive home. I'll let Bill tell you what happened:

> As we were driving along, we were excited, and I, like any sixteen-year-old driver, was probably not paying enough attention to my speed. Just as we were turning on the cloverleaf to get on the expressway, I will never ever, ever forget watching that sewing machine, which was already top-heavy, begin to tip. I slammed on the brakes, but it was too late. I saw it go over the side. I jumped out and ran around the back of the truck. As I rounded the corner, I saw our hope and our dream lying on its side in pieces. And then I saw my dad just looking. All of his risk and all of his endeavor and all of his struggling and all of his dream, all of his hope to take care of his family was lying there, shattered.
>
> You know what comes next, don't you? "Stupid, punk kid driving too fast, not paying attention,

ruined the family by taking away our livelihood."
But that's not what he said. He looked right at
me. "Oh, Bill, I am so sorry." And he walked over,
put his arms around me, and said, "Son, this is
going to be okay."[6]

God is whispering the same to you. Those are his
arms you feel. Trust him. That is his voice you hear.
Believe him. Allow the only decision maker in the universe to comfort you. Life at times appears to fall to
pieces, seems irreparable. But it's going to be okay. How
can you know? Because *God* so loved the world. And,

> Since he has no needs, you cannot tire him.
> Since he is without age, you cannot lose him.
> Since he has no sin, you cannot corrupt him.

If God can make a billion galaxies, can't he make
good out of our bad? Of course he can. He is God. He
not only flies the plane, but he knows the passengers and
has a special place for those who are sick and ready to get
home.

Becca, 17

When I thought one of my friends had stolen my favorite DVD, I didn't handle it too well. I should have trusted her and asked her before I accused her. But I didn't. Later I found the DVD under the car seat.

It's like that with God too. Sometimes I forget to trust God because I'm in a hurry to fix it all by myself. Remembering to ask for God's help is something I struggle with a lot, and so do my friends.

It's hard to believe when people all around you tell you he is not real and that believing is useless. Then again, something deep inside me tells me it's true. And that he's always listening when I whisper, "God, can we talk?"

THINK IT OVER

Who is God to you?

_____
_____
_____
_____

Think about a tough time in your life. How did it make you feel about God?

_____
_____
_____
_____

What one thing in God's creation points you to him more than anything else?

_____
_____
_____
_____

3

Does God love everyone?

> **3:16—"For God so loved *the world* . . ."**

In the movie *The Sandlot*, The Babe offers this advice: "Heroes get remembered, but legends never die. Follow your heart, kid, and you'll never go wrong."

It's a nice thought, but the tragic truth is that it doesn't work this way when hearts are hard. Hard hearts lead to wrong wants . . . and, well, their actions speak for themselves.

"I look at this people—oh! what a stubborn, hard-headed people" (Exodus 32:9 MSG). God spoke these words to Moses on Mount Sinai. The disloyalty of the calf-worshiping Hebrews shocked God. He had given them a front-row seat at his Exodus extravaganza. They saw water transform into blood and high noon change to a midnight sky. The Red Sea turned into a red carpet, and the Egyptian army became fish bait. God gave manna with the morning dew, quail with the evening sun. He earned their trust. The former slaves had witnessed amazing miracles like they had never seen.

And yet, when God called Moses to a mountaintop meeting, the people panicked. "They rallied around Aaron and said, 'Do something. Make gods for us who will lead us. That Moses, the man who got us out of Egypt—who knows what's happened to him?'" (32:1 MSG).

Fear infected everyone in the camp like a case of contagious chicken pox. They crafted a metal cow and talked to it. God, shocked at the calf-praising service, commanded Moses, "Go! Get down there! . . . They've turned away from the way I commanded them. . . . Oh! what a stubborn, hard-headed people!" (32:7–9 MSG).

Note: The presence of fear in the Hebrews didn't bother God; their response to it did. Nothing made the people trust him. Plagues didn't. Freedom from slavery didn't. God shed light on their path and dropped food in their laps, and still they didn't believe him. Nothing penetrated their hearts. Mount Rushmore is more pliable, an anvil more tender. The people were as responsive as the gold statue they worshiped.

More than three thousand years later, we understand God's frustration. Turn to a statue for help? We opt for more classy cures: belly-stretching food binges or budget-busting shopping sprees. Progress? Hardly. We still face fears without facing God.

He sends Exodus-sized demonstrations of power: sunsets, starry nights, immeasurable oceans. He solves Red Sea–sized problems and airdrops blessings like morning manna. But let one problem show up, let Moses disappear for a few hours, and we are a mess. Rather than turn to God, we turn from him, hardening our hearts. The result? Cow-worshiping foolishness.

Becca, 17

Cow-worshiping really makes worshiping stuff other than God and not trusting him look dumb. It halfway makes me want to laugh at them, but then again I think that we all have a bit of cow-worshiping in our lives. I suppose, that's the problem of sin.

When I get scared—I'm ashamed to say—I turn from God, and instead of worshiping a calf, I usually swear or say mean things to people. It's not right, and it's not okay. It's just not trusting the Lord that he is watching over and protecting me.

> Please, Lord, I ask that you will help me to trust you. I feel so ashamed of myself sometimes because I know you are there for me, but I do not always turn to you. I will never understand why you chose me and why you love me, but I am glad you do.

My friend Karen Hill saw the result of stubbornness like that of the Israelites. A cow in a pasture stuck her nose into a paint can and couldn't shake it off. Can-nosed cows can't breathe well, and they can't drink or eat at all. Both the cow and her calf were in danger. A serious bovine bind.

Karen's family set out to help. But when the cow saw the rescuers coming, she ran for pasture. They followed, but the cow escaped. They chased that cow for three days! Each time the posse drew near, the cow ran. Finally, using pickup trucks and ropes, they cornered and de-canned the cow.

Seen any can-nosed people lately? Hungry souls? Thirsty hearts? People who can't take a deep breath? All because they stuck their noses where they shouldn't, and when God came to help, they ran away.

When billions of us imitate the cow, chaos erupts.

TIME FOR REFLECTION

Sometimes do you stick your nose where you shouldn't . . .

a. to feel better about yourself by hearing about someone else's mistakes?

b. because if you don't keep up with the gossip this week, you won't know what's happening next week?

c. to know which kids to stay away from?

d. because you're bored?

e. because you're there?

Next time you're tempted to stick your nose where you shouldn't, picture in your mind . . .

a. a canned-nose cow.

b. hard-hearted Israelites.

c. God's love that comes around even when you're stuck.

d. All of the above.

Nations of bull-headed people avoiding God and bumping into each other. We scamper, starve, and struggle.

Can-nosed craziness. Isn't this the world we see? This is the world God sees.

Yet, this is the world God loves. "For God so loved the world . . ." This hard-hearted, stiff-necked world.

We bow before gold-plated cows; still, he loves us.

We stick our noses where we shouldn't; still, he pursues us.

We run from the very one who can help, but he doesn't give up.

And what does heaven think about our recklessness?

[Hard-hearted people] are hopelessly confused. Their minds are full of darkness; they wander far from the life God gives because they have closed their minds and *hardened their hearts against him*. They have no sense of shame. They live for lustful pleasure and eagerly practice every kind of impurity. (Ephesians 4:17–19 NLT; emphasis added)

Did you catch that?

- "Hopelessly confused"
- "Minds . . . of darkness"
- "Have no sense of shame"
- "Live for lustful pleasure"
- "Practice every kind of impurity"

No wonder Scripture says, "He who hardens his heart falls into trouble" (Proverbs 28:14).

Justin, 16

It's so easy to be blinded by the darkness of the world. I know, 'cause good is not the norm in my world. Most of my friends don't think twice about doing wrong things. And they especially don't call those things sin. Even if they did, it's not like they'd stop anyway. They do what they do 'cause they like it. They are so focused on themselves, they rarely—if ever— think about what's good or right.

Sometimes I feel like I'm surrounded by stubborn, hard-hearted people. To even do something kind can put me "out there." Still, I befriended a guy not in the group. And my friends looked at me like I'd lost my mind. To retaliate, my friends "forgot" to pick me up for a concert that night. I'd worked for a long time to get the money for my ticket, and I had already paid for it and couldn't get a refund. They made me feel really rotten about doing the right thing, yet I still think I made the right choice.

BC—Before Christ was in my life—I thought doing the right things would be easy, but now I understand that it's not. I know God is trying to mold me. No pain, no gain.

He loves. He pursues. He persists. And every so often, a heart starts to soften.

Let yours be one of them. Here's how:

Don't forget what God has done for you. Jesus performed two bread-multiplying miracles: in one he fed five thousand people, in the other four thousand. Still, his disciples, who witnessed both feasts, worried about empty lunch boxes. An annoyed Jesus scolded them: "Are your hearts too hard to take it in? . . . Don't you remember anything at all?" (Mark 8:17–18 NLT).

> ## HOLDING ON TO SIN HARDENS US. CONFESSION SOFTENS US.

Short memories harden the heart. Make careful note of God's blessings. Declare with David: "[I will] daily add praise to praise. I'll write the book on your righteousness, talk up your salvation the livelong day, never run out of good things to write or say" (Psalm 71:14–15 MSG).

Take time to write down God's goodnesses. Meditate on them. He has fed you, led you, and earned your trust. Remember what God has done for you. And then:

Acknowledge what you have done against God. "If we claim we have not sinned, we are calling God a liar and showing that his word has no place in our hearts" (1 John 1:10 NLT).

Holding on to sin hardens us. Confession softens us.

When my daughters were small, they liked to play with Play-Doh. They formed figures out of the soft clay. If they forgot to place the lid on the can, the substance hardened. When it did, they brought it to me. My hands were bigger. My fingers stronger. I could mold the stony stuff into putty.

Is your heart hard? Take it to your Father. You're only a prayer away from tenderness. You live in a hard world, but you don't have to live with a hard heart.

THINK IT OVER

Why do you think people are so forgetful about the good things God does?

_____

_____

_____

_____

_____

_____

_____

What happened the last time you (or a friend) stuck your nose where you shouldn't?

_____

_____

_____

_____

_____

_____

_____

When was a time when "being good" made you not fit in?

_____

_____

_____

_____

_____

_____

_____

_____

4

Why does God love us?

> 3:16—"For God so *loved* the world . . ."

Pluto got bumped, cut from the first team, moved down from the top nine. According to a committee of scientists meeting in Prague, this far-out planet fails to meet solar-system standards. They downgraded the globe to asteroid #134340.[1] Believe me, Pluto was not happy. I caught up with the dissed sky traveler at a popular constellation hangout, the Night Sky Lounge.

MAX: Tell me, Pluto, how do you feel about
              the decision of the committee?

PLUTO: You mean those planet-pickers from Prague?

MAX: Yes.

PLUTO: I say no planet is perfect. Mars looks like a tanning-bed addict. Saturn has rings around the collar, and Jupiter moons everyone who passes.

MAX: So you don't approve of the decision?

PLUTO: (*snarling and whipping out a newspaper*) Who comes up with these rules? *Too small. Wrong size moon. Not enough impact.* Do they know how hard it is to hang on at the edge of the solar system? They think I'm spacey. Let them duck meteors coming at them at thousands of miles per hour for a few millennia, and then see who they call a planet. I'm outta here. I can take the hint. I know when I'm not wanted. Walt Disney named a dog after me. Teachers always put me last on the science quiz. Darth Vader gives me more respect. I'm joining up with a meteor shower. Tell that committee to keep an eye on the night sky. I know where they live.

Can't fault Pluto for being ticked. One day he's in, the next he's out; one day on the squad, the next off. We can understand his frustration. Some of us understand it all too well. We know what it's like to be voted out. Wrong size. Wrong crowd. Wrong address.

Plutoed.

To the demoted and demeaned, Jesus directs a powerful verb. "For God so *loved* the world . . ." *Love.* We've all but worn out the word. This morning I used *love* to describe my feelings toward my wife and toward peanut butter. Far from identical emotions. I've never proposed to a jar of peanut butter (though I have let one sit on my lap during a television show).

Scripture employs an artillery of terms for love, each one calibrated to reach a different target. Consider the one Moses used with his followers: "The LORD chose your ancestors as the objects of his love" (Deuteronomy 10:15 NLT).

This passage warms our hearts. But it shook the Hebrews' world. They heard this: "The Lord binds [*hasaq*] himself to his people." *Hasaq* speaks of a tethered love, a love attached to something or someone.[2] I'm picturing a mom connected by a child harness to her rambunctious five-year-old as the two of them walk through the market. (I once thought the leashes were cruel; then I became a dad.) The strap serves two functions, yanking and claiming. You yank your kid out of trouble and in doing so proclaim, "Yes, he is as wild as a banshee. But he's mine."

RANDOM THOUGHTS

Plutoed—a new term for being rejected/
cut off. (Did Mickey ever put Pluto
on a leash?)

Leash—once for dogs, now used for kids,
for protection.

Protection—When I accept Jesus, God binds
me to him. He doesn't let go. It's
for forever.

Maybe if the planet Pluto had a leash, we
wouldn't be having this talk about whether it
belongs or not.

In the case of Israel, God chained himself to them. Why did God love? Because the people were lovable? No. "GOD wasn't attracted to you and didn't choose you because you were big and important—the fact is, there was almost nothing to you. He did it out of sheer love, keeping the promise he made to your ancestors" (Deuteronomy 7:7–8 MSG). God loves Israel and the rest of us Plutos because he chooses to. "This is the love that won't let go of the object of love."[3]

Becca, 17

I was Plutoed yesterday by one of my best friends. He's a guy, and like most of us, Zach has an ego to protect—so he ditched me to hang with one of his "cool" friends. It wasn't fair. It stunk even more when I discovered the friend he ditched me for doesn't like me. I felt like Zach was embarrassed by me. That I wasn't good enough. It hurt.

I wanted to tell someone, but if I told my other friends . . . would they ditch me too? I didn't say anything. Instead, I tucked the sting deep inside, and I hid behind a smile. No one likes a whiner, but for some reason I feel it's okay to bring these things to God, right? He knows how I feel.

Lord, often I think that nobody will ever love me because I don't feel special, but then I think of your love—it's forever. If you, the most important person in the universe, love me, then why wouldn't others? Your love gives me hope.

God will not let you go. He has handcuffed himself to you in love. And he owns the only key. You need not win his love. You already have it. And since you can't win it, you can't lose it.

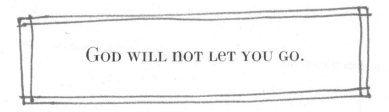

GOD WILL NOT LET YOU GO.

I know a father who, out of love for his son, spends each night in a recliner, never sleeping more than a couple of consecutive hours. A car accident paralyzed the teenager. To maintain the boy's circulation, therapists massage his limbs every few hours. At night the father takes the place of the therapists. Though he's worked all day and will work again the next, he sets the alarm to wake himself every other hour until sunrise.

Then there is the story Dan Mazzeo tells about his father: "Pop," a first-generation Italian American who was struggling with liver and lung cancer. When doctors gave him less than a year, Pop bravely said he wasn't afraid to die. After all, his wife was already gone and his children were grown. But then he learned that his only son, Dan, was going to be a father. When Pop heard the news, he sat up and resolved, "I'm gonna make that."

The chemo tortured his system. Some days it was all

he could do to mumble, "Bad day" to those who phoned. But when his granddaughter was born, he insisted on going to the hospital. The ninety-minute ride pained him. Dan wheeled him to the maternity ward. Pop's arms were too weak, so Dan had to hold the baby for him. But Pop did what he came to do. He leaned over, kissed her, and said, "Sheila Mary, Grandpa loves you very much."

Within seconds, Pop dozed off. Within an hour, he was back in the car. Within days, he was dead.[4]

What is this love that passes on sleep and resists death to give one kiss? Call it agape love, a love that bears a semblance of God's.

But only a semblance, mind you, never a replica. Our love doesn't even come close to God's. Our finest love is a preschool watercolor to God's masterpiece. It's a vacant-lot dandelion next to his garden rose.

We may issue a final blessing, but compare our love with God's? Look at the round belly of the pregnant peasant girl in Bethlehem. God's in there; the same God who can balance the universe on the tip of his finger floats in Mary's womb. Why? Love.

Peek through the Nazareth workshop window. See the lanky lad sweeping the sawdust from the floor? He once blew stardust into the night sky. Why swap the heavens for a carpentry shop? One answer: love.

Love explains why he came.
Love explains how he endured.

His hometown kicked him out. A so-called friend turned him in. Sinners called God guilty. How did Jesus endure such derision? "For God so loved . . ."

"Observe how Christ loved us. . . . He didn't love in order to get something from us but to give everything of himself to us" (Ephesians 5:2 MSG).

Your goodness can't win God's love. Nor can your badness lose it. But you can resist it. We tend to do so honestly. Having been Plutoed so often, we fear God may Pluto us as well. Rejections have left us skittish and jumpy. Like my dog Salty.

> ## YOUR GOODNESS CAN'T WIN GOD'S LOVE.

He sleeps next to me on the couch as I write. He's a cranky cuss, but I like him. He didn't have much to start with; now the seasons have taken his energy, teeth, hearing, and all but eighteen inches' worth of eyesight.

Toss him a dog treat, and he just stares at the floor through cloudy cataracts. (Or, in his case, dogaracts?) He's nervous and edgy, quick to growl and slow to trust. As I reach out to pet him, he yanks back. Still, I pet the old coot. I know he can't see, and I can only wonder how dark his world has become.

We are a lot like Salty. We are anxious folk—can't see a step into the future, can't hear the one who owns us. No wonder we try to gum the hand that feeds us.

But God reaches and touches. He speaks through the immensity of the Russian plain and the density of the Amazon rain forest. Through a physician's touch in Africa, a bowl of rice in India. He's even been known to touch people through paragraphs like the ones you are reading. If he is touching you, let him.

Mark it down: God loves you with an unearthly love. You can't win it by being charming. You can't lose it by being a loser. But you can be blind enough to resist it.

Don't. For heaven's sake, don't. For your sake, don't.

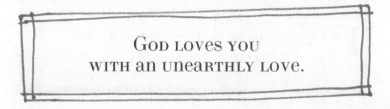

GOD LOVES YOU
WITH AN UNEARTHLY LOVE.

"Take in with all followers of Jesus the extravagant dimensions of Christ's love. Reach out and experience the breadth! Test its length! Plumb the depths! Rise to the heights! Live full lives, full in the fullness of God" (Ephesians 3:18–19 MSG). Others undervalue you. God claims you. Let the ultimate voice of the universe say, "You're still a part of my plan."

Justin, 16

Sometimes I wonder how I fit into God's plan. For years my life has looked more like one of those mazes than a straight line. I never knew which direction to turn or where I'd end up. But last year, when I asked Jesus to take over my life, things started changing. Not overnight like I hoped, but slowly.

I still make bad decisions and take wrong turns. Sometimes I feel a little lost, but overall I feel better. My life means something. I have a spot, a purpose. I'm so glad God doesn't give up and boot me out. He's holding on to me, and his forever kind of love is the best.

THINK IT OVER

Have you ever been Plutoed? If so, what did you do?

_____

_____

_____

_____

How does it feel to know you're never a loser in God's book?

_____

_____

_____

_____

Think about God's plan. In what ways do you fit into his plan? In what ways are you still waiting to discover your perfect place?

_____

_____

_____

5

What's the big deal about Jesus?

3:16—". . . he gave his *one and only Son* . . ."

For a while we lived in the North Zone of Rio de Janeiro, Brazil. On the other side of the mountain, in the South Zone, were important places we had to visit—like the hospital where two of my daughters were born.

We didn't complain about the drive through a tunnel to the other side of the mountain. The only problem was, I kept getting lost. I'm directionally challenged anyway. I'm known to take a wrong turn between the bedroom and bathroom. Throw in three-hundred-year-old streets that seemed to be placed wherever-they-pleased, and I didn't stand a chance.

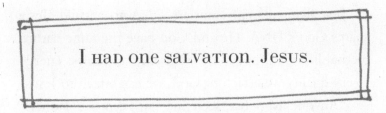

I HAD one SALVATION. JESUS.

I had one salvation. Jesus. Honestly, Jesus. A statue of Christ the Redeemer. The figure stands guard over the city, one hundred twenty-five feet tall with an arm span of nearly a hundred feet. More than a thousand tons of reinforced steel. The head alone measures ten feet from chin to scalp. Standing a mile and a half above sea level, Jesus is always visible. Especially to those who are looking for him.

Since I was often lost, I was often looking. As a sailor seeks land, I searched for the statue, looking between the phone lines and rooftops for the familiar face. Find Jesus and find the right direction.

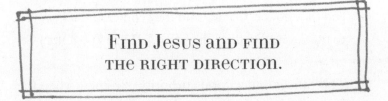

FIND JESUS AND FIND THE RIGHT DIRECTION.

John 3:16 offers the same promise. The verse lifts Christ up and crowns him with a royal name: "One and Only Son."

Other translations say "only begotten Son" (John 3:16 NKJV, NASB). Begotten? Like "born"? Not really. It means something more.

Just like a parent transfers DNA to a child, Jesus shares God's DNA. He and God have the same nature, eternal life span, unending wisdom, and tireless energy. Every quality we attach to God, we can attach to Jesus.

"Anyone who has seen me has seen the Father!" Jesus claimed (John 14:9 NLT).

Jesus accepted this fact. He claims, not the most authority, but all of it. Listen to this:

> A Roman officer sent a message to Jesus, asking the teacher to heal his servant. So Jesus journeyed toward the soldier's house. But the man sent friends to stop Jesus, telling him that trip wasn't needed. "Just say the word from where you are, and my servant will be healed. I know this because I am under the authority of my superior officers, and I have authority over my soldiers. I only need to say, 'Go,' and they go, or 'Come,' and they come. And if I say to my slaves, 'Do this,' they do it." (Luke 7:7–8 NLT)

This officer understood authority. He knew when the one in charge commands, the ones beneath obey. The soldier was stating, "Jesus, you call the shots. You own the throne." He saluted Christ as supreme commander.

And Christ didn't correct him! He could have said, "You flatter me." Instead, Jesus knew someone finally got it. Can you imagine Jesus's excitement: "I tell you, I haven't seen faith like this in all Israel!" (Luke 7:9 NLT).

Justin, 16

I wish my faith was always as strong as the soldier's faith, but God knows it doesn't even come close. Sometimes (and I think God understands this) the only way for me to know what I feel is to get my guitar and sing. It may sound crazy, but . . . hey, it works. Below is something I wrote to remind myself that people and things draw my heart, but only God satisfies my heart. Only God should rule the space deep in my heart.

Lookin' for somethin' to fill love's
    void,
My heart thought it found a jewel.
She believed my words were just a
    game.
Shoulda stuck to lovin' you.

Sin led me down a different way,
Telling me I was a fool.
God called me back to the only
    right path.
Shoulda stuck to lovin' you.

Steer my heart,
Steer my life,

As—only you can.
I'm breathin'
I'm needin',
More—of your plan.

I put God in the driver's seat.
Tired of this long, lonely road.
Toss my plans out the window,
Takin' the path that leads home.

I walked alone in the wrong
    direction,
You, God, called to me still.
Your path, not mine, dear Lord.
Your hand guidin' my will.

Steer my heart,
Steer my life,
As—only you can.
I'm breathin'
I'm needin',
More—of your plan.

No seekin' love just to please me,
    Lord.
No sin guiding my way.
You, God, are what truly matters.
You, alone all of my days.

Christ steers the ship and pilots the plane. When he darts his eyes, oceans swell. When he clears his throat, birds migrate. He banishes bacteria with a single thought. "He sustains everything by the mighty power of his command" (Hebrews 1:3 NLT).

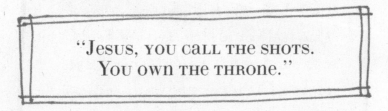

"JESUS, YOU CALL THE SHOTS.
YOU OWN THE THRONE."

Thinking of what he does with history reminds me of what a weaver does with tapestry. I once watched a weaver work at a downtown San Antonio market. She selected threads from her bag and arranged them first on the frame, then on the shuttle. She next worked the shuttle back and forth over the threads, intertwining colors, overlapping textures. In a matter of moments a design appeared.

Christ, in a similar way, weaves his story. Every person is a thread, every moment a color, every era a pass of the shuttle. Jesus steadily interweaves the embroidery of humankind. "'My thoughts are nothing like your thoughts,' says the LORD. 'And my ways are far beyond anything you could imagine'" (Isaiah 55:8 NLT). A root meaning of the word translated "thoughts" is "artistic craftsmanship."[1] As if God says, "My artistry is far beyond anything you could imagine."

Becca, 17

I wonder why God and his son chose this time in history to put me here? Why this city, this family, this school? When I was a kid, my favorite books were stories of people crossing the prairie in covered wagons. Sure they had problems, but they were things like bears and raging rivers. I deal with raging thoughts. I let my mind wander too much—like with thoughts of cool movie stars. Or that cute guy, Brandon, who sits in front of me in history class. I talked with my mom about it, and she said she struggles with her thoughts too. Not about the same stuff, but other temptations and worries in life. She says prayer helps her turn her thoughts back where they belong.

So I tried it. I prayed and asked God to help. Sometimes I still find myself staring at Brandon, and I wonder what it would be like to kiss him. If I know I'm gonna see him, I take extra time styling my hair and picking out my clothes. I replay in my mind every comment he makes, looking for any hint that he likes me. It's enough to drive me crazy! If only I thought about God as much . . . then maybe my life would be different, easier.

But my mom also said that if the struggles in my life make me turn to God, then maybe those struggles have a purpose. I do pray more, and I think about what's right instead of just letting my mind run wild. So maybe there's another reason Brandon's seated in front of me . . . . so I can turn to God, learn to control my thoughts, and discover God and his son's love in new ways. Now there's a thought I really like!

Jesus enjoys an intimacy with God, a mutuality the Father shares with no one else. "No one really knows the Son except the Father, and no one really knows the Father except the Son" (Matthew 11:27 NLT).

> EVERY PERSON IS A THREAD,
> EVERY MOMENT A COLOR, EVERY
> ERA A PASS OF THE SHUTTLE.

Jesus not only knows God, he tells us about him. Jesus "who exists at the very heart of the Father, has made him plain as day" (John 1:18 MSG).

When Jesus says, "In My Father's house are many mansions" (John 14:2 NKJV), count on it. He knows. He has walked them.

When he says, "You are worth more than many sparrows" (Matthew 10:31), trust him. Jesus knows. He knows the value of every creature.

> # Heaven's DOOR HAS one KEY, anD JESUS HOLDS IT.

When Christ declares, "your Father knows the things you have need of" (Matthew 6:8 NKJV), believe it. After all, "He was in the beginning with God" (John 1:2 NKJV).

Heaven's door has one key, and Jesus holds it.

Think of it this way: You're a fifth grader studying astronomy. The day you read about the first mission to the moon, you and your classmates pepper the teacher with space-travel questions.

"What does moon dust feel like?"

"Can you swallow when there's no gravity?"

"What about going to the bathroom?"

The teacher does the best she can but prefaces most replies with "I would guess . . ." or "I think . . ." or "Perhaps . . ."

How could she know? She's never been there. But the next day she brings a guest who has. Neil Armstrong enters the room. Yes, the "one small step for man, one giant leap for mankind" Neil Armstrong.

"Now ask your questions," the teacher invites. And Astronaut Armstrong answers each with sureness. He knows the moon; he's walked on it. No guessing—he speaks out of experience. So did Jesus.

Jesus knows the dimensions of God's throne room, the favorite songs of the unceasing angel choir. He has a unique, one-of-a-kind knowledge of God. He wants to share his knowledge with you. "No one really knows the Father except the Son and those *to whom the Son chooses to reveal him*" (Matthew 11:27 NLT; emphasis added).

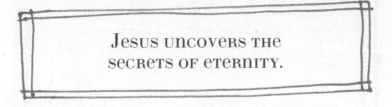

JESUS UNCOVERS THE
SECRETS OF ETERNITY.

Jesus doesn't boast in what he knows; he shares it. Jesus uncovers the secrets of eternity.

And he shares them, not just with the smart and important people, but with the hungry and needy. In the very next line, Jesus invites: "Come to me, all of you who are weary and carry heavy burdens, and I will give you rest. Take my yoke upon you. Let me teach you, because I am humble and gentle at heart, and you will find rest for your souls" (Matthew 11:28–29 NLT).

Read that again: "Let me teach you . . ."

Justin, 16

Sometimes life seems like a pop quiz, which isn't always a bad thing. I've been learning more about God's love . . . which I'm discovering is more about HIM than me. See how well you do on the quiz below.

GOD LOVES ME
QUIZ

Answer the following questions by circling True or False. (If you are uncertain, check the Scripture verses.)

GOD LOVES ME BECAUSE . . .

1. I am perfect inside and out, without a flaw. [True/False] Romans 3:23-25

2. He sees me as his wonderful creation. [True/False] Genesis 1:27-31

3. I always choose to do the right things and choose the right friends. [True/False] 1 John 1:8

4. He has decided to be my friend, when I was his enemy. [True/False]
   Romans 5:8

5. I show my family what living for Jesus looks like day and night. [True/False]
   Psalm 37:23-24

6. Jesus lived in the bounds of day and night to show me he was the way.
   [True/False] Hebrews 5:7-9

7. I make all the right decisions concerning my life. [True/False] Romans 3:10

8. He made the decision to offer me life through his death. [True/False]
   John 3:16

How well did you do on this quiz? The answers are F/T/F/T/F/T/F/T. Remember: Let Jesus continue to teach you.

Years ago, one of my Boy Scout assignments was to build a kite. One of my blessings as a Boy Scout was a kite-building dad. He built a lot of things: scooters on skates, go-carts. Why, he even built our house. A kite to him was stick figures to Van Gogh. Dad could build one in his sleep.

With wood glue, poles, and newspaper, we made a

sky-dancing masterpiece: red, white, and blue, and shaped like a box. We launched our creation on the back of a March wind. But after some minutes, my kite caught a downdraft and hit the ground.

Picture a redheaded, heartsick twelve-year-old standing over his broken kite. That was me. Imagine a square-bodied man with ruddy skin and coveralls, placing his hand on the boy's shoulder. That was my kite-making dad. He looked at the heap of sticks and paper and gave me hope: "It's okay. We can fix this." I believed him. Why not? He spoke with authority.

> TO ALL WHOSE LIVES FEEL LIKE a CRASHED KITE, JESUS SAYS, "We can FIX THIS. LET me TEACH YOU."

So does Christ. To all whose lives feel like a crashed kite, Jesus says, "We can fix this. Let me teach you." Let me teach you how to handle your after-school job, Monday pop quiz, and pesky sister. Let me teach you why people fight, bad things happen, and forgiveness counts. But most of all, let me teach you why on earth you are on this earth.

We need answers. Jesus offers them.

But can we trust him? Only one way to know. Do what I did in Rio. Seek him out. Lift up your eyes. No passing glances. Focus on Jesus.

You'll find more than the right road.
You'll find the Only One and Only.

Becca, 17

Jesus says, "Let me teach you," but sometimes I think I'll never learn. When I was a kid, I sang "Jesus loves the little children, all the children of the world, red and yellow, black and white . . . ," but sometimes I forget all means all.

The weird thing is, I understand that Jesus loves the poor people, but it's harder to remember he loves the beautiful people and the ones who seem to have it all. Like Marni, the new girl in youth group. I didn't talk to her—no one really did. Then, one night at youth camp, I heard her crying herself to sleep. I felt awful! The next morning I made a point to talk to her, and I found out we had a lot of stuff in common. In fact, she had a lot more struggles than I thought . . . bad grades, fighting with her mom all the time, and losing her best friend in a skiing accident. I could tell she felt alone and needed someone to care.

I don't know what came over me, but suddenly I got really bold. I told her we don't have to be alone. We all can have a hand to hold. And that God loves everyone . . . her, and me, and everyone.

Hey, maybe I am learning! Thanks, God!

THINK IT OVER

When your life felt like a crashed, broken kite, how did Jesus help you fix it?

In what ways have you allowed God to steer your heart? How has the new heart-direction also steered your actions?

....

....

....

....

....

Has there ever been someone in your life who you thought had it "all together" and later found out they didn't? What hope can you offer that person?

....

....

....

....

....

Do you ever struggle with "all means all" when it comes to God's love? Why?

....

....

....

....

....

6

Why did Jesus die for us?

3:16—". . . he *gave* his one and only Son . . ."

I didn't think much of my too-fast pulse, especially when a bowl of ice cream was involved. But when the doctor put the words *irregular* and *heartbeat* together, I was concerned. It was the random rhythms that worried the cardiologist. You won't find a kinder physician. He did his best to promise me that, as far as heart conditions go, mine isn't serious.

Forgive the fact I didn't jump for joy. But isn't that like telling the about-to-leap paratrooper, "Your parachute has a defect, but it's not the worst type"?

I prefer the treatment of another heart doctor. He

saw my problem and made this eye-popping offer: "Let's exchange hearts. Mine is sturdy; yours is weak. Mine pure, yours diseased. Take mine and enjoy its strength. Give me yours. I'll endure its irregularity." Where do you find such a physician? You can reach him at this number—3:16. At the heart of this verse, he deals with the heart of our problem: "For God so loved the world that he *gave* his one and only Son."

> "LET'S EXCHANGE HEARTS. Mine IS STURDY; YOURS IS WEAK."

"That's the craziest claim I've ever heard," a man once told me. He and I shared a row and a meal on an airplane. But we did not share an appreciation for John 3:16.

"I don't need God to *give* anyone for me," he claimed. "I've led a good life. Held a good job. People respect me. I don't need God to give me his son."

Perhaps you agree. You appreciate the teachings of Jesus. Admire his example. But no matter how you turn it around, you can't see the significance of his death. How can the death of Christ mean life for us? The answer begins with a heart exam.

"The heart *is* deceitful above all *things*, and desperately wicked" (Jeremiah 17:9 NKJV).

The Spiritual Cardiologist scans our hearts and finds

deep disease: "No one is righteous—not even one. No one is truly wise; no one is seeking God" (Romans 3:10–11 NLT).

Justin, 16

I confess, God. There is dark stuff in my heart I've never told anyone about, like the trouble I have with cussing. I pray it gets better, but sometimes it slips. I feel horrible when that happens.

Then there are other things I'm not as eager to give up. It's not like I want to enjoy sin—but there are thoughts I like to let roll. Like replaying in my mind the photos I ran across on the Internet. Or the scenes from a movie I knew I shouldn't have watched, but did. The truth is, I don't always want to stop sinning. If sin is so bad, why does it sometimes feel so good? Sometimes I wonder how I got here in the first place. Help me, God!

This generation is oddly silent about sin. But all of us have it. If our hearts were an apple, the sin inside would be the worm eating it away.

How does a worm get inside an apple? Perhaps you

think the worm burrows in from the outside. No, scientists have discovered that the worm comes from inside. But how does he get in there? Simple! An insect lays an egg in the apple blossom. Sometime later, the worm hatches in the heart of the apple, then eats his way out. Sin, like the worm, begins in the heart and works out through a person's thoughts, words, and actions.[1]

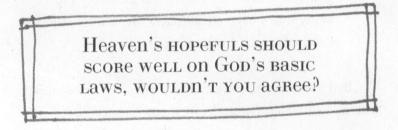

> Heaven's HOPEFULS SHOULD
> SCORE WELL ON GOD'S BASIC
> LAWS, WOULDN'T YOU AGREE?

Our heart problem? It's universal.

And personal. Do a simple exercise with me. Measure *your* life against these four standards from the Ten Commandments. Heaven's hopefuls should score well on God's basic laws, wouldn't you agree?

1. "You must not steal" (Exodus 20:15 TLB). Have you ever stolen anything? A soft drink, a test answer? Thief.

2. "You must not lie" (Exodus 20:16 TLB). Those who say they have never lied just did.

3. "Honor your father and mother" (Exodus 20:12 TLB). I'm not even going to ask. But just so we're clear, honor means obey. You can add

Colossians 3:20: "You children must always obey your fathers and mothers, for that pleases the Lord" (TLB).

4. "You must not murder" (Exodus 20:13 TLB). Before you claim innocence, remember, Jesus equates murder with anger. "Anyone who is so much as angry with a brother or sister is guilty of murder" (Matthew 5:22 MSG). How many times have we all been angry with others—family, friends, and even strangers.

Bad news from the doctor. Your test score indicts you as a thieving, lying, disobedient murderer.

Compare your heart with Christ's. He claimed to have the only sinless heart in all of history. He asked, "Can any one of you convict me of a single misleading word, a single sinful act?" (John 8:46 MSG).

> ## JESUS'S PERFECT SCORE ALLOWS NO ROOM FOR BOASTING.

If I asked my friends that question, hands would raise. But no one could convict Jesus of sin. His enemies made up false charges in order to arrest him.

Pilate, the highest-ranking official in the region, found no guilt in Jesus. Peter, who walked in Jesus's shadow for three years, wrote: "He never did one thing wrong, not once said anything amiss" (1 Peter 2:22 MSG).

Jesus's perfect score allows no room for boasting.

Becca, 17

My heart looks sick, sick, sick compared to Jesus's perfect score. I can't even manage to treat everyone the same. Sometimes I rank people before I even realize I'm doing it. And, depending on who I'm around, my view of myself even changes. Sometimes I'm at the end of the list, like when I'm not wearing the same type of clothes everyone else is at the Friday night game. Sometimes I'm at the top when I'm feeling really good about myself, like when I changed my plans to help my mother by baby-sitting my little cousin all day. I'm not alone either. We all rank each other and ourselves.

I know God loves me, but sometimes I wonder how he loves me just as much as everyone else . . . equally. It's not like anyone else can love everyone equally. I need to remind myself that Jesus loves me because he can't help it. It's the same with his love for everyone else too. He made us; we are his.

When my puppy, who is dearest to me in the world, chewed up my favorite shoes, all I had to do was look into his eyes and see the cute, funny, and adorable creature underneath. I think that's the same with Jesus. He sees us through eyes of love. He's the perfect doctor for my sick heart . . . if only I can remember to seek his help for my unholy thoughts and comparisons!

So how does Jesus respond to our unholy hearts? Can a good doctor spot a heart problem and ignore it? Can God overlook our sins as innocent mistakes? No. He is the one and only judge. He issues orders, not opinions; commands, not suggestions. They are truth.

Jesus made his point clear: "Anyone whose life is not

> Can a GOOD DOCTOR SPOT a
> HEART PROBLEM AND IGNORE IT?

holy will never see the Lord" (Hebrews 12:14 NCV). Hard-hearted souls will not populate heaven.

It is the "pure in heart" who will "see God" (Matthew 5:8). So where does that leave us? Christ exchanged hearts with you. Yes, your thieving, lying, disobeying, and murderous heart. Jesus placed your sin in himself and invited God to punish it. "The LORD has put on him the punishment for all the evil we have done" (Isaiah 53:6 NCV).

> ## JESUS PLACED YOUR SIN IN HIMSELF AND INVITED GOD TO PUNISH IT.

A Chinese Christian understood this point. Before her baptism, a pastor asked a question to ensure she understood the meaning of the Cross. "Did Jesus have any sin?" he inquired.

"Yes," she replied.

Troubled, he repeated the question.

"He had sin," she answered positively.

The leader set out to correct her, but she insisted, "He had mine."[2]

Though healthy, Jesus took our disease upon himself. Though diseased, we who accept his offer are pronounced healthy. We are declared innocent.

We enter heaven not with healed hearts but with *his* heart. It is as if we have never sinned. Read slowly the

69

words of Paul: "If anyone is in Christ, he is a new creation; the old has gone, the new has come!" (2 Corinthians 5:17).

> We enter heaven not with healed hearts but with HIS heart.

This is no transplant, mind you, but a swap. The holy and the horrid exchange places. God makes healthy what was sick. Right what was wrong.

There is a Spanish story of a father and son who had a bitter argument. The son ran away, and once he was gone, the father realized his loss. In hopes of finding him, the father posted a sign at the busiest store in town: "Paco, come home. I love you. Meet me here tomorrow morning." The next day seven Pacos, who had also run away from home, showed up looking for their fathers. They were all answering the call for love, each hoping it was his dad inviting him home with open arms.[3]

Are you looking for what those Pacos were—for the wrong to be made right?

"Can you do something with this heart?" we ask.

He nods and smiles. "Suppose we discuss a swap."

Becca, 17

Sometimes I think to myself, I can't deal with this heart.
But instead of just thinking I know it's time to pray.

God, can you help me, please? I know you
can see beneath all the grime, dirt, lies, and hate.
I'm sorry for all the pain I've caused you. I
give you all my angry thoughts, hatred, guilty
conscience, lazy flesh. Can I get everything of
you, God, in return? Can you make my wrongs
right? Yes? Wow, what a swap!

I can feel a difference in my heart . . . . for now.
But sometimes I forget my heart has been swapped.
That's why I'm going to make a list. Maybe I'll put it on
my mirror. Maybe even my locker too.

> ## Ten Things to Remind Me
> ## of My God-Swapped Heart!

1. A swapped heart knows God.
   "Be still, and know that I am God." Psalm 46:10

2. A swapped heart prays.
   "Do not be anxious about anything, but in everything by prayer and petition, with thanksgiving, present your requests to God." Philippians 4:6

3. A swapped heart looks to Jesus.
   Picture Jesus in the storm. See Jesus quieting the waves.

4. A swapped heart sees where Jesus sits.
   "Let us fix our eyes on Jesus, the author and perfecter of our faith, who for the joy set before him endured the cross, scorning its shame, and sat down at the right hand of the throne of God."
   Hebrews 12:2

5. A swapped heart puts someone else first.
   "May I help you with that? How may I serve?"

6. A swapped heart surrenders.
   "Lord, my life is in your hands."

7. A swapped heart thanks God.
   "All the good I do is because of you. Thank you!"

8. A swapped heart trusts in God's protection.
   "Be my rock of refuge, to which I can always go;
   give the command to save me, for you are my rock
   and my fortress." Psalm 71:3

9. A swapped heart cares more for people than things.
   "You matter to me. . . ."

10. A swapped heart knows where to turn when
    temptation comes.
    "Lord, help me!"

Why did Jesus die for us?

THINK IT OVER

Do you have a God-swapped heart?

_____
_____
_____
_____

What problems has sin caused in your life?

_____
_____
_____
_____

How does God help you in your struggles with sins you don't want to give up?

_____
_____
_____
_____

7

What is God's "whoever" policy?

> 3:16—". . . *whoever* believes in
> him shall not perish . . ."

Cleopatra's Needle juts from the ground like a tall pencil—complete with a pointy top. The Egyptian monument stands out like the foreigner she is in London. Her engravings speak of a different time in history and use an ancient language. Workers constructed the obelisk 3,500 years ago as a gift for an Egyptian pharaoh. But on September 12, 1878, the British government planted it in English soil, giving it a spot by the Thames River.

F. W. Boreham was there. He was seven years old the day his father and mother took him on the train to

London to witness the moment. He described the "great granite column, smothered with its maze of hieroglyphics." He watched the relic rise "from the horizontal to the perpendicular, like a giant waking and standing erect after his long, long sleep."

His father explained the importance of the structure: how it once guarded a great temple. Pharaohs passed it in their chariots. Moses likely studied on its steps. And now, protected by stone sphinxes, Cleopatra's Needle overlooked a river in London . . . with a time capsule buried in her base.

The city officials believed that some day the box might be opened to find a piece of Victorian England. If so, the person would discover a set of coins, children's toys, a city directory, photographs of the twelve most beautiful women of the day, a razor, and, in 215 languages, a verse from the Bible: "For God so loved the world that he gave his one and only son, that whoever believes in him shall not perish but have eternal life."[1]

Can you picture someone in future London digging through rocks and rubble? She finds and reads the verse. Except for one word, she might think it's just a myth. *Whoever.*

Whoever speaks to future London just like it did to the 1878 crowd. Just like it does to us. *Whoever* invites the world—past, present, and future—to God.

Jesus could have so easily changed *whoever* into *what-*

WHOEVER makes it clear: GOD OFFERS HIS GRACE ALL OVER THE WORLD.

ever. "Whatever Jew believes" or "Whatever woman follows me." He didn't. Who isn't a *whoever?*

Whoever makes it clear: God offers his grace all over the world. For anyone who tries to leave others out, Jesus has a word: *Whoever.*

God's *Whoever* Policy
(emphasis added)

Whoever acknowledges me before men, I will also acknowledge him before my Father in heaven. (Matthew 10:32)

Whoever finds his life will lose it, and *whoever* loses his life for my sake will find it. (Matthew 10:39)

Whoever does God's will is my brother and sister and mother. (Mark 3:35)

Whoever believes and is baptized will be saved, but *whoever* does not believe will be condemned. (Mark 16:16)

Whoever believes in the Son has eternal life, but *whoever* rejects the Son will not see life, for God's wrath remains on him. (John 3:36)

Whoever drinks the water I give him will never thirst. (John 4:14)

Whoever comes to me I will never drive away. (John 6:37)

Whoever lives and believes in me will never die. (John 11:26)

Whoever is thirsty, let him come; and *whoever* wishes, let him take the free gift of the water of life. (Revelation 22:17)

Paul states that Jesus Christ "sacrificed himself to win freedom for all mankind" (1 Timothy 2:6 NEB). God's gospel has a "whoever" policy. All means all.

Becca, 17

I spotted a cross today, hanging around the neck of a rapper singing with a cheeseburger in his hand for some goofy commercial. I know the type of music the guy sings. I've heard about the type of life he lives. He wears the cross because he thinks it looks good, but he's missing the whole point. He's like a living oxymoron. He wears the sign of salvation and forgiveness, but he lives like he wants to: without rules and, worst of all, without God.

I've never done anything as bold before, but I imagined walking up to him and asking "Nice cross. What does it mean?"

Problem was, I then imagined someone asking me the same thing.

I clicked off the TV and knew what I had to do. I bought a cross on a chain to wear. To me it takes on two meanings:

1) if I'm doing something worthy of my calling people know who to credit, and

2) if I'm not being a good example, it weighs on me and reminds me of who I'm living for.

Thank you, Jesus, for what you did on the Cross, not only for me, but for whoever—all who believe. May I always remember that what is a symbol for us cost you your life. And that's serious stuff.

We know about the *whoever*. At least most of the time we remember. Sometimes, though, life gets so hard we wonder if God still wants us.

> ONCE-POOR LAZARUS NOW NEEDS NOTHING. THE NOW-POOR RICH MAN NEEDS EVERYTHING.

Surely Lazarus the beggar wondered. (Not the Lazarus Jesus raised from the dead, but a different one Jesus told a story about.) Listen to this:

There was a rich man who was dressed in purple and fine linen and lived in luxury every day. At his gate was laid a beggar named Lazarus, covered with sores and longing to eat what fell from the rich man's table. Even the dogs came and licked his sores. (Luke 16:19–21)

The two men live on opposite sides of the city tracks. The rich man lives in luxury and wears the finest clothing. The language suggests he uses fabric worth its weight in gold.[2] He eats the best food, enjoys a mansion with gardens and a pool. He's the New Testament version of a Hollywood billionaire.

Lazarus is a homeless bum. Dogs lick the sores that

cover his skin. He hangs around outside the mansion, hoping for leftovers dumped in the trash. Infected. Rejected. Nothing but the clothes on his back. No family. Surely God doesn't include him in the "whoever" policy, right?

Wrong.

> The time came when the beggar died and the angels carried him to Abraham's side. The rich man also died and was buried. In hell, where he was in torment, he looked up and saw Abraham far away, with Lazarus by his side. (Luke 16:22–23)

Once-poor Lazarus now needs nothing. The now-poor rich man needs everything. He loses the lap of luxury, and Lazarus discovers the lap of Abraham.

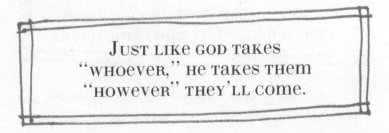

JUST LIKE GOD TAKES
"WHOEVER," HE TAKES THEM
"HOWEVER" THEY'LL COME.

People like Lazarus still populate our planet. You may be one. Not begging for bread, but struggling to scrape together lunch money. Not sleeping on streets, but on the floor perhaps? On a couch often?

If this story has you thinking, don't miss the main

point: God takes you *however* he finds you. You don't need to clean up or become more important. Just like God takes "whoever," he takes them "however" they'll come.

Just don't forget the "whenever."

Whenever you hear God's voice, he welcomes your response.

While cleaning my car, I found a restaurant gift certificate. Hidden in the papers, gum wrappers, and trash was a treasure: fifty dollars worth of food! I'd received it for my birthday over a year ago and had misplaced it. My excitement didn't last long. The expiration date had passed. I had waited too long. But you haven't.

If you're alive, it's not too late.

> THOSE WHO LIVE FOR JESUS
> THEIR WHOLE LIVES AND THOSE WHO
> ACCEPT HIM WITH THEIR LAST BREATH
> ENTER HEAVEN BY THE SAME GATE.

Jesus made it clear with this story: He described a landowner who needed helpers and so he hired a crew. "They agreed on a wage of a dollar a day, and went to work" (Matthew 20:2 MSG). A few were hired early in the morning. Others at 9:00 a.m. The landowner hired a few more at noon. Came back at 3:00 p.m. for more. And at 5:00 p.m., one hour before quitting time, he picked up one more truckload.

Those last men were surely surprised. One hour remaining in the workday . . . how much should they expect? No one pays a day's wage to one-hour workers, does he?

God does.

Read Jesus's punch line: "They got the same, each of them one dollar" (Matthew 20:10 MSG). Those who live for Jesus their whole lives and those who accept him with their last breath enter heaven by the same gate.

Justin, 16

Sometimes I have a hard time thinking that ax murderers who say a prayer right before they're zapped in the electric chair can make it to heaven just like the old lady who lived her whole life taking care of orphans in Africa. So I decided to start a list of all the things people should have done to be saved.

If I Were God, Who Would I Save?

- People who read the Bible.
- People who read . . . and agree . . . with the Bible.

- Church people.
- People who pray more than only at dinnertime.
- Those who can recite the 10 Commandments from memory.
- Those who obey "the Golden Rule" by always treating others as they would want to be treated themselves.
- People who think about God through the week, not just on Sundays.
- People who aren't shy about witnessing to others.
- Volunteers for stuff like feeding the homeless.
- People who never gossip.

Whoa, wait a minute . . . this list means I wouldn't make it to heaven. Nor would some really good people I know.

Thank you, God, for your "whoever" policy. It's a good thing that "whosoever believes in Jesus" is all that you require to enter heaven. Otherwise, heaven would be a pretty empty place because no one would be good enough.

And one more point I have to add on: *whoever* means "wherever." *Wherever* you are, you're not too far to come home.

The prodigal son thought he was. (And if you're curious like I was, *prodigal* means wasteful, reckless, and uncontrolled. Not what you'd call a "cautious" guy.) He had walked away from his father's kindness and "journeyed to a far country, and there wasted his possessions with prodigal living" (Luke 15:13 NKJV).

> ## WHEREVER YOU ARE, YOU'RE NOT TOO FAR TO COME HOME.

The word translated here as *wasted* is the same one used to describe a farmer throwing seeds. Picture a farmer tossing handfuls of seeds onto tilled earth. In the same way, the son tosses his father's money to anyone who promises a fun time: a roll of bills at one arcade, a handful of coins at another. He rides the magic carpet of cash from one party to the next.

And then one day his wallet grows thin. The credit card comes back. The hotel clerk says "no," the hotel says "go," and the boy says "uh-oh." He slides from high hog to low pig in the mud. He gets a job feeding swine.

The hunger is so great he considers eating with the pigs. Instead, he swallows his pride and begins that famous walk home, practicing how he'd ask for his father's forgiveness. Turns out he didn't need to. "His father saw him and had compassion, and ran and fell on his neck and kissed him" (Luke 15:20 NKJV). The father was saving the son's place.

He's saving yours too. If heaven's banquet table has nameplates, one bears your name.

> IF HEAVEN'S BANQUET TABLE HAS NAMEPLATES, ONE BEARS YOUR NAME.

We lose much in life—our temper, our cash, our parents' approval. We lose opportunities and chances, and we lose at love. We lose youth and misplace dreams. We lose much, but we never lose our place on God's "whoever" list.

Whoever—God's wonderful word of welcome.

I love to hear Denalyn say "whoever." Sometimes I note my favorite fragrance coming from the kitchen: strawberry cake. I follow the smell like a bird dog follows a trail until I'm standing over the just-baked, just-iced

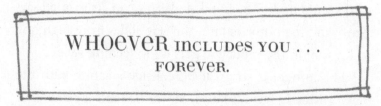

> WHOEVER INCLUDES YOU . . .
> FOREVER.

pan of pure pleasure. Yet I've learned to still my fork until Denalyn gives clearance.

"Who is it for?" I ask.

She might break my heart. "It's for a birthday party, Max. Don't touch it!"

Or, "For a friend. Stay away."

Or she might throw open the door of delight. "Whoever." And since I qualify as a "whoever," I say "yes."

I so hope you will too. Not to the cake, but to God.

No status too low.

No hour too late.

No place too far.

However. Whenever. Wherever.

Whoever includes you . . . forever.

Becca, 17

I didn't have a date for the senior prom, but the invitation told me I didn't need one. My friend Hailey and I went together. My dress was blue. Hers was black and white, and we felt like two princesses. Even my hair turned out perfect, and I told the hairdresser I wish she could meet me at my house before school every day!

Hailey and I met up with other friends. We waved at everyone we recognized and even those we didn't . . . like two princesses would. Some people had dates but others, like us, just went with a friend. All were welcome—the popular students, the ordinary ones, and those like me in between.

Tonight I experienced a glimpse of what God means by whoever. All who accepted the invitation came. We were welcomed into a beautiful hall filled with metallic balloons that reflected the glimmering miniature lights. And we all laughed and talked and enjoyed the fun. Perfect.

Thanks, God, for allowing me to be one of whoever . . .

THINK IT OVER

Why do you think we judge who we think should (or shouldn't!) make it to heaven?

_____

_____

_____

_____

_____

How does it make you feel to know you'll never lose your place on God's "whoever" list?

_____

_____

_____

_____

_____

What does the Cross mean to you in your everyday life?

_____

_____

_____

_____

_____

What does it mean to believe?

3:16—". . . whoever *believes* in him shall not perish . . ."

Tell me my part again," I groaned.

"Just trust me," she assured. *She* was a bubbly, college-aged, baseball-capped, rope holder. *Trust me* meant taking a backward leap off a fifty-foot cliff, wearing a belay harness and a what-did-I-get-myself-into expression.

Some people love rappelling. They live for the stomach-in-the-throat feeling. Not me. I prefer the seat-in-the-chair one. I had traveled to Colorado to experience a week of rest to the fullest. Fresh air, great views. Good coffee, long talks. These events made my list. Jumping backward off the mountain didn't.

Blame pesky friends and stupid pride for my place on
the peak. They promised a safe landing.

"Ever done this?" the girl asked.

"No."

She handed me a leather harness and told me to step
in. "It's kind of like a diaper." She smiled, all too chipper.

I may need a diaper, I thought.

"What about you?" I inquired. "Have you lowered
anyone down the mountain?"

"Been working here all summer." She beamed.

It was barely July.

"It's simple," she continued as she clipped me in and
handed me gloves. "Hold the rope and jump. Bounce
off the wall with your feet."

I decided there should be a new law—the words
jump, bounce, and *wall* should never be spoken in the
same breath.

"How do I keep from crashing?"

"You don't. I do that."

"You?"

"Yes, I hold your rope."

That gave me little comfort. Not only was she half
my age, she was half my size.

"But don't I do *something?*" I begged.

"You trust me."

I inched up to the edge of the cliff and looked down.
Frodo felt safer looking into the pit.

"Do you have any valuables?" I heard a voice ask.

"Only my life."

"You're funny," she chirped, sounding so much like my daughters that I remembered my will was out-of-date. "Come on. It's your turn!"

Jesus's invitation seems too simple.

I gave her one more look. A look that some people give me when I tell them about 3:16. I can see it in their eyes: Can I really trust that "whoever *believes* in him shall not perish"?

Jesus's invitation seems too simple. We want to choose other verbs. *Work* has a better ring to it. "Whoever works for him will be saved."

Pleases fits nicely. "Whoever pleases him will be saved." But believe? *Shouldn't I do more?*

Justin, 16

I haven't told many people that I'm afraid of heights. You won't see me jumping off a mountain—no matter how big the rope. I'm also afraid of failing chemistry and not making enough money this summer to get

---

my own car. Then there is the idea of really messing up in front of others and getting embarrassed. Doesn't that scare everyone?

I like it best when my life is in control. But it rarely is. I think it started with my parents' divorce. Nothing I could do made it better. Maybe now I go overboard in trying to control everything. Since no one can do that, I usually end up feeling like a big fat failure.

The future is like one big question mark. When I think about the next five years, I get an ache in the pit of my stomach like that one time I rode a roller coaster. I hated every minute of it, but once I was seatbelted in, I had to go along for the ride.

That's what school and life feel like. I have no idea what I want for my future. I know I don't want to hate my job like my dad does. Or cry over money all the time like my mom.

I need answers, but I'm afraid to ask for help. It's hard to trust people. Sometimes it's even hard to trust God. Still, there's something inside me that wonders:
Shouldn't I do more?

Wanting to do more seems to be the struggle of Nicodemus. It was his conversation with Christ, remember, that set the stage for John 3:16. What Nicodemus asked Jesus was the same I asked the take-a-leap girl . . . What's my part?

> ### WHAT NICODEMUS ASKED JESUS WAS THE SAME I ASKED THE TAKE-A-LEAP GIRL . . . WHAT'S MY PART?

The baby doesn't do anything to be born. The infant allows the parent to do the work. Salvation is equally simple. God works and we trust. Such a thought troubles Nicodemus. *There must be more.* Jesus comforts the visiting professor with an account from the Torah, Nicodemus's favorite book.

> And as Moses lifted up the bronze snake on a pole in the wilderness, so the Son of Man must be lifted up, so that everyone who believes in him will have eternal life. (John 3:14–15 NLT)

Nicodemus knew this event. A one-sentence reference was enough for him to understand the point. The verse is cryptic to us, however. Why did Jesus precede the 3:16 offer with a reference to a serpent in the wilderness? Here is the backstory.

The wandering Israelites were grumbling at Moses again. Though camped on the border of the Promised Land and beneficiaries of four decades of God's provisions, the Hebrews sounded off like spoiled trust-fund brats: "Why have you brought us up out of Egypt to die in the wilderness?" (Numbers 21:5 NKJV).

Same complaint, seventieth verse. Ex-slaves longing for Egypt. Dreaming of pyramids and cursing the wasteland, pining for Pharaoh and vilifying Moses. They hated the hot sand, the long days, and the manna, oh the manna. "Our soul loathes this worthless bread" (21:5 NKJV).

They'd had all the manna burgers and manna casseroles and manna peanut butter sandwiches they could stomach. And God had had all the moaning he could take. "So the LORD sent fiery serpents among the people, and they bit the people; and many of the people of Israel died" (21:6 NKJV).

Horror-movie producers long to spawn such scenes. Slithering vipers creep out of holes and rocks and serpentine through the camp. People die. Corpses dot the landscape. Survivors pleaded with Moses to plead with God for mercy. "'We have sinned. . . . Pray to the LORD that He take away the serpents from us.' So Moses prayed for the people. Then the LORD said to Moses, 'Make a fiery serpent, and set it on a pole; and it shall be that everyone who is bitten, when he looks at it, shall live.' So Moses made a bronze serpent, and put it on a pole; and so it was, if a serpent had bitten anyone, when he looked at the bronze serpent, he lived" (21:7–9 NKJV).

This passage was a solemn prophecy.

And it was also a simple promise. Snake-bit Israelites found healing by looking at the pole. Sinners will find healing by looking to Christ. "Everyone who believes in him will have eternal life" (John 3:15 NLT).

The simplicity troubles many people. We expect a more complicated cure, a more elaborate treatment. Moses and his followers might have expected more as well. Manufacture an ointment. Invent a therapeutic lotion. Treat one another. Or at least fight back. Break out the sticks and stones and attack the snakes.

We, too, expect something to do. We want to know what will help us fix our sin problem. Some mercy seekers have donned hair shirts, climbed cathedral steps on their knees, or traversed hot rocks on bare feet. Ouch!

Becca, 17

I never really thought about people trying to fix their own sin problem, but I guess it makes sense. This became real to me when my own cousin had problems forgiving herself after a car accident. I prayed for her, but then I knew I had to do more. So I wrote her. I hope it helps!

Dear Amber,

Thanks for writing and telling me what happened . . . about the car accident. I hope your friend will be okay. Well, let me change that. I know she'll never be like she used to be, and I imagine not being able to walk would change things. But I'm glad she didn't die. I'd hate for you to live the rest of your life knowing that your drinking and driving caused someone to die. What happened is bad enough.

It seems like forever since we talked. I remember sitting in that blow-up pool in the backyard and seeing how long we could hold our breath under water. I think you won. I wish life was that simple still . . . that we could just laugh and play without thinking of serious stuff.

I've been thinking of a lot more serious things lately—like reading about Jesus's sacrifice on the cross. And about John 3:16. I think about what it must have been like for Jesus to live perfectly without sinning and then to feel the sin of the whole world on him. No wonder he felt forsaken!

In your letter, you said you felt Jesus could never

forgive you for what happened. That broke my heart! But I've been thinking . . . if we tell Jesus there are things, no matter what they are, that we don't feel he can forgive, then maybe we're telling him the Cross wasn't good enough. It seems to me that people drink alcohol to stop feeling . . . but Jesus felt it all as he died. He felt the pain so you could feel forgiveness. Just something to think about.

Mind if I pray for you?

Dear Jesus, I pray for my cousin. Be with her during the very hard stuff. Just like you offered the gift of forgiveness, strengthen her to accept it. There is nothing we can ever do in our own power to earn your forgiveness; accepting is all you ask. Thank you, Lord. Amen.

Okay, write me. Maybe we can get together this summer, but instead of counting the seconds we can stay under the water, we can count the good things Jesus has done for us. And remember . . . God wants to help us. He knows we can't fix ourselves.

Have you ever heard: "God helps those who help themselves"?

We'll fix ourselves, thank you. We'll make up for our mistakes by helping others or giving extra. We'll make up for our guilt with staying busy for God. We'll overcome failures with hard work. We'll find salvation the old-fashioned way: we'll earn it.

Christ believes just the opposite. He says to us what the rope-holding girl said to me: "Your part is to trust. Trust me to do what you can't."

By the way, you take similar steps of trust daily, even hourly. You believe the chair will support you, so you set your weight on it. You believe water will hydrate you, so you swallow it. You trust the work of the light switch, so you flip it. You have faith the doorknob will work, so you turn it.

> YOU REGULARLY TRUST POWER YOU CANNOT SEE TO DO A WORK YOU CANNOT ACCOMPLISH. JESUS INVITES YOU TO DO THE same WITH HIM.

You regularly trust power you cannot see to do a work you cannot accomplish. Jesus invites you to do the same with him.

Just him. Not any other leader. Not even yourself. You can't fix you. Look to Jesus . . . and believe.

Remember my rappelling partner? She told me to fix my gaze on her. As I took the plunge, she shouted, "Keep your eyes up here!" I didn't have to be told twice. She was the only one of the two of us smiling.

But since she did her work, I landed safely. Next trip, however, you'll find me in a chair on the porch.

Becca, 17

"Trust me". . . sometimes I cringe when I hear those words. I've tried that. There are some things I can't trust, like crossed fingers and toes. I can't trust my school board, my neighbor's dog, or my cell phone to not drop a call. Sometimes I trust. Just last week I trusted my friend with my favorite shirt, and she ruined it. I trusted my boyfriend . . . gave him too much of myself, and he dumped me a week later.

Then again, even though others let me down, I know I can trust you, Jesus. At church I hear things like you're my Lord, Savior, Redeemer, Strong Tower, Refuge, and Strength, but I like to think of more practical things. You're my Savior because you saved me from sin. Some days everyone seems to be against me, but I know I can always turn to you to protect and care for me. You're my strength because there are times I get so tired of all the hard things, yet when I pray I feel as if I've just been given an energy drink for the heart. Thank you, God. All these things remind me again how YOU can be trusted.

THINK IT OVER

When was a time you found it hard to trust Jesus to do what you couldn't on your own? Did you finally learn to trust? What was the result?

_____

_____

_____

_____

_____

What does it mean to believe?

How does knowing about what Jesus did on the Cross then help you now?

_____

_____

_____

_____

_____

Was there ever a time you did something that you felt God could never forgive you for? How have you learned to trust him?

_____

_____

_____

_____

_____

9

What can a person do to become a Christian?

> **3:16—". . . whoever believes**
> ***in him* shall not perish . . ."**

Team Hoyt consists of a father-son squad: Dick and Rick. They race. They race a lot. Sixty-four marathons (26.2 miles each). Two hundred and six triathlons (6.2 miles of running, 56 miles of bicycling, and .9 miles of swimming). Six triathlons at Ironman distance (26.2 miles of running, 112 miles of bicycling, and 2.4 miles of swimming). Two hundred and four 10K runs. Since 1975, they've crossed nearly a thousand finish lines. They've even crossed the USA. It took them forty-five days to run and pedal 3,735 miles, but they did it.

Team Hoyt loves races. But only half of Team Hoyt

can run. Dick, the dad, can. But Rick's legs don't work; nor does his speech. At his birth in 1962, the umbilical cord wrapped around his neck, starving oxygen from his brain, stealing movement from his body. Doctors gave no hope for his development.

Dick and his wife, Judy, disagreed with the doctor's prognosis. He couldn't bathe, dress, or feed himself, but he could think. They knew he was bright. So they enrolled him in public school. He graduated. He entered college and graduated again.

> He couldn't bathe, dress, or feed himself, but he could think.

But Rick wanted to run. At age fifteen, he asked his dad if they could enter a five-mile benefit race. Dick was not a runner, but he was a father, so he loaded his son in a three-wheeled wheelchair, and off they went. They haven't stopped since.

Young Rick Hoyt depends on his dad to do it all:

lift him,

push him,

pedal him,

and tow him.

Other than a willing heart, he makes no contribution to the effort. Rick depends entirely on the strength of his dad.[1]

God wants you to do the same. "Whoever believes *in him* shall not perish but have eternal life" (John 3:16).

The phrase "believes *in him*" doesn't digest well. "Believe *in yourself*" is the common menu choice of our day. Try harder. Work longer. Dig deeper. "Do it myself" is our goal.

Becca, 17

They call this the human race, but sometimes I wonder what everyone is racing for? Good grades, the right boyfriend/girlfriend, getting into the right college, the highest score on the video game, the coolest skateboard tricks, getting into a size zero jeans? Personally, I just want a nice, sensitive guy, good grades, a family that doesn't fight, money for a car, good friends, and a college scholarship. Is that too much to ask? Hmmm...

I wonder what my friends expect to find at the end of the race? Or what I hope for? I've been there before. I strive for something and then as soon as I "arrive" it's not what I thought it would be.

Lord, can you give me a boost—and help me race toward more faith? I know this means putting more trust into what you're up to, than what I can do in my own strength. I'm learning that faith is being lifted, pushed, pedaled, and towed . . . and relying totally on you. It's a very humbling place to be, but I suppose once I start feeling the wind on my face . . . as Jesus carries me forward . . . I'll never want to try to do it on my own again!

How come people in the human race work so hard to do it themselves? Doesn't "in him" seem easier?

"In him" smacks of leaving out all other ways. Don't all paths lead to heaven? Islam, Hinduism, Buddhism, and humanism? Salvation comes in many forms, right? Christ says "no." Salvation is found *in him*.

We bring to the spiritual race what Rick Hoyt brings to the physical one. Our spiritual legs have no strength. Our honor has no muscle. Our good deeds cannot carry us across the finish line, but Christ can. "To the one who does not work, but believes *in Him* who justi-

fies the ungodly, his faith is credited as righteousness"
(Romans 4:5 NASB; emphasis added).

In that verse above, Paul promises salvation to the most
unlikely folks. Not to the one who works, but to the
trust-er. Not to the fit, but to the weak. Not to the wealthy
and powerful saint, but to the poor and unemployable—
the child who will trust with Rick Hoyt trust.

> ## OUR GOOD DEEDS CANNOT CARRY US ACROSS THE FINISH LINE, BUT CHRIST CAN.

This verse says it all: "Trusting-him-to-do-it is what
gets you set right with God, *by* God. Sheer gift" (Romans
4:5 MSG; emphasis added).

We bring what Rick brings. And God does what Dick
does. He takes start-to-finish-line responsibility for his children. "I give them eternal life, and they shall never perish;
no one can snatch them out of my hand" (John 10:28).

> ### Justin, 16
>
> "Trust in Jesus" seems too simplistic. I've got serious stuff to worry about.

- My mom wanting to move out of state away from my dad.
- My knee injury that could make me sit on the bench.
- A shooter entering my school and being helpless to do anything to stop him.
- What in the world I'm going to do after high school.
- GIRLS.

It's not like I'm always obsessed about these worries, but they're always there, buzzing around my mind like mosquitoes at a summer picnic. Part of me says it's okay to worry. That it's only human and it helps me prepare and not be surprised when bad things happen. But another part tells me the more I worry about stuff, the more I see those things as bigger than God.

I'm learning more about this thing called faith, and to me it means believing that none of these things are more powerful than God—in my life and in my mind. I don't have to rely on my ability to change. In fact, I can't change one thing on my worry list. When things get too tough, I don't have to worry about what steps to take; God will carry me from start to fin-ish . . . for real.

An air force pilot told me of the day he forgot to buckle himself into the seat of his jet.

The jet was made so that once it was in the air, the belt couldn't be buckled. He could either ride it out or eject from the plane. If he ejected, his seat wouldn't come with him . . . and the seat held the parachute. Think face-plant at 120 mph. That'll suck the joy out of the trip. Can you imagine flying a jet without a parachute?

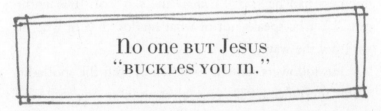

No one BUT JESUS
"BUCKLES YOU IN."

Many do. Eternal insecurity extracts joy from many people. Only Christ guarantees a safe landing. Parallel his offer with that of other religions. Judaism sees salvation as a Judgment Day decision based on morality. Hindus anticipate multiple reincarnations in the soul's journey through the cosmos.[2] Buddhism grades your life according to the Four Noble Truths and the Noble Eightfold Path. Muslims earn their way to Allah by performing the duties of the Five Pillars of Faith.[3] Many philosophers deem life after the grave as hidden and unknown. One called death a step into "the great Perhaps"[4]; another, "a great leap in the dark."[5]

No one but Jesus "buckles you in." You may slip—indeed you will—but you will not fall. Jesus wants you to believe "in him." Don't believe in you; you can't save you. And don't believe in others; they can't save you.

Some historians clump Christ with Moses, Muhammad, Confucius, and other spiritual leaders. But Jesus refuses to share the page. He declares, "I am the way, and the truth, and the life; no one comes to the Father, but by me" (John 14:6 RSV).

He could have scored more points in political correctness had he said, "I *know* the way" or "I *show* the way." Yet he speaks not of what he does but of who he is: I *am* the way.

His followers refused to soften or shift the spotlight. Peter announced: "There is salvation in no one else! God has given no other name under heaven by which we must be saved" (Acts 4:12 NLT).

Still, we worry what others will think about this announcement. The world doesn't seem as big as it did fifty years ago. We have friends from all over the globe. Many of them believe in different things.

Maybe we shouldn't make such a big deal out of Jesus's claim. Instead, can't we just say that all roads lead to heaven?

But can they?

Islam says Jesus was not crucified. Christians say he was. Both can't be right.

Judaism refuses the claim of Christ as the Messiah.[6] Christians accept it. Someone's making a mistake.

Spiritists read your palms. Christians consult the Bible.

Somebody is wrong.

And, most importantly, every non-Christian religion says, "You can save you." Jesus says, "My death on the cross saves you."

How can all religions lead to God when they are so different?

We don't pretend that all roads lead to London or all ships sail to Australia. All flights don't land in Rome. Imagine what you would say to a travel agent who claims they do. You tell him you need a flight to Rome, Italy, so he looks on his screen.

"Well, there is a flight to Sydney, Australia, departing at 6:00 a.m."

"Does it go to Rome?"

"No, but it offers wonderful meals and movies."

"But I need to go to Rome."

"Then let me suggest Southwest Airlines."

"Southwest Airlines flies to Rome?"

"No, but they've won many awards for on-time arrivals."

You're getting a little fed up. "I need one airline to carry me to one place: Rome."

The agent acts offended. "Sir, all flights go to Rome."

You know better. Different flights go different places. Every flight does not go to Rome. Every path does not lead to God. Jesus blazed a stand-alone trail void of self-salvation. He cleared a one-of-a-kind passageway uncluttered by human effort. Christ came not for the strong but for the weak; not for the righteous but for the sinner. We enter his way upon confession of our need, not completion of our deeds. He offers a unique-to-him invitation in which he works and we trust, he dies and we live, he invites and we believe.

> EVERY FLIGHT DOES NOT GO TO Rome.
> EVERY PATH DOES NOT LEAD TO GOD.

We believe *in him*. In Jesus. "The work God wants you to do is this: Believe the One he sent" (John 6:29 NCV).

Believe in yourself? No. Believe in him.

Believe in them? No. Believe in him.

And those who do, those who believe "in him shall not perish but have eternal life" (John 3:16).

How do we begin to believe? We do what young Rick Hoyt did. We turn to our Father for help.

When Dick and Rick Hoyt cross finish lines, both receive finisher medals. The list of people who finish the race includes both names. The dad does the work, but the son shares in the victory. Why? Because he believes. And because he believes, both celebrate the finish.

May you and your Father do the same.

Becca, 17

I've had a bad feeling in the pit of my gut lately, mostly because some of my friends are so religious. That sounds like a good thing right? Wrong. Not when you believe in the wrong thing.

I had one girl I worked with at the coffee shop tell me I'm intolerant, narrow-minded, because I believe that Jesus is the only way to heaven. Then there is my friend Michelle who says she believes in God, but not Jesus.

I know what I know—not just with my mind, but deep in my soul. For as long as I remember I've been told that being a Christian means accepting Jesus, believing he is God's son, and committing your life to him. I did this and I know God is real, just as I know my own name.

Thankfully, I have Kate, My Accountability Partner from my youth group. Or as we call each other, we're MAPs. She's someone who's there to remind me that I am doing and believing the right things, no matter what others think. In the Bible, Jesus sent his disciples out in pairs. Now I know why. It's good to have a friend there to whine to, to talk with, and to tell you, "Yeah, I know. It's hard, but let's pray."

THINK IT OVER

If a friend were to ask you, "What can I do to become a Christian?" what would you say?

_____

_____

_____

_____

People are always on the run. How are you sure that you are running toward anything that will make an eternal difference?

_____

_____

_____

_____

Do you ever struggle with people who think there are "many ways to get to heaven"? What do you tell them?

_____

_____

_____

_____

10

Won't everyone be in heaven?

3:16—"... whoever believes in him shall not *perish*..."

The hero of heaven is God. Angels don't worship mansions or glittering streets. Neither gates nor jewels prompt the hosts to sing . . . God does.

The people of heaven are always amazed by sins God forgives. The promises he keeps. The plans he carries out.

God's blockbuster movie has a single showing, with a solo star: himself. He invites every living soul to attend. To everyone he calls out, "Come, enjoy me forever."

Yet many people don't want anything to do with God. He speaks, and they cover their ears. He offers instructions; they laugh at them. They don't want him telling them how to live.

> GOD'S BLOCKBUSTER MOVIE
> HAS A SINGLE SHOWING, WITH
> A SOLO STAR: HIMSELF.

They mock what he says about marriage, money, sex, or the value of human life. They regard his son as a joke and the Cross as utter folly.[1] Some people spend their lives telling God to leave them alone. And at the moment of their final breath, he does: "Get away from me, you who do evil. I never knew you" (Matthew 7:23 NCV). This verse talks about something no one wants to speak about: hell.

> SOME PEOPLE SPEND THEIR
> LIVES TELLING GOD TO LEAVE THEM
> ALONE. AND AT THE MOMENT OF
> THEIR FINAL BREATH, HE DOES.

It's easy to understand why. Hell is an ugly topic.

The people who wrote the Bible speak of the "blackest darkness" (Jude 1:13), "of everlasting destruction" (2 Thessalonians 1:9), "of weeping and gnashing of teeth"

(Matthew 8:12). Not something fun to chat about with a friend.

Someone did talk about it a lot . . . Jesus. He used one key word to warn us: *perish.* "Whoever believes in him shall not *perish* but have eternal life" (John 3:16, emphasis added).

Jesus spoke of hell often. Thirteen percent of his teachings refer to eternal judgment and hell.[2] Two-thirds of his parables relate to resurrection and judgment.[3] Jesus wasn't cruel or capricious, but he was blunt. His candor stuns.

> EXACTLY WHERE IS HELL? JESUS GIVES ONE SCARY CLUE: "OUTSIDE."

He speaks in tangible terms. "Fear Him," he warns, "who is able to destroy both soul and body in hell" (Matthew 10:28 NKJV). He quotes Hades's rich man pleading for Lazarus to "dip the tip of his finger in water and cool my tongue" (Luke 16:24 NKJV). Words such as *body, finger,* and *tongue* presuppose a physical state in which a throat longs for water and a person begs for relief—physical relief.

Exactly where is hell? Jesus gives one scary clue: "outside."

"Tie him hand and foot, and throw him *outside,* into the darkness" (Matthew 22:13; emphasis added).

Outside of what? Outside of the boundaries of heaven, for one thing. No heaven-to-hell field trips. No hell-to-heaven holiday breaks. Heaven is not reachable from hell.

The apostle John talks about what's waiting for the wicked in Revelation 14:11: "The smoke of their torment goes up forever and ever, and they have no rest, day or night" (ESV).

Jesus describes the length of heaven and hell with the same adjective: *eternal*. "They will go away into eternal punishment, but the righteous into eternal life" (Matthew 25:46 RSV).

> MANY THINGS DIE IN HELL.
> HOPE DIES. HAPPINESS DIES.

Hell lasts as long as heaven. There is no end. It may have a back door or graduation day, but I haven't found it.

Many things die in hell. Hope dies. Happiness dies. But the body and soul of those who tell God to "keep away" continues. There they stay—outside of heaven, outside of hope, and outside of God's goodness.

We can't even imagine it. Even bad people on earth enjoy good things. They hear children laugh. They smell dinner cooking. They tap their toes to the beat of a good song. They deny God yet enjoy his gifts.

Justin, 16

I've heard horrible rumors about people at school, yet nothing they've done seems as bad as knowing they are going to hell. Sometimes I think it would be nice if hell were a horrible rumor.

It makes me think about something I heard in youth group: "We can say, 'THY will be done,' or 'MY will be done.'" Then, when we stand before God, he'll remind us of our choice. His desire would be that no one goes to hell—and that all would believe what he has to say. Instead, people like to believe what they think about God, or what they've heard from people who spout their own ideas.

I suppose I've told rumors, too, about other people, thinking I was being funny. At the time I didn't realize how damaging it really could be to someone's feelings, reputation, and social life. And I've had rumors said about me too. I remember trying to tell people that what was being spread about me wasn't true, but nobody listened. It makes me think how God must feel when we don't believe him when his word talks about serious stuff like hell.

> I know where I'm going after I die;
> that's what matters. My job is to take as
> many people to heaven with me as I can.

In hell people can be as ugly as they want. Hunger for evil will run free. People who worry will fuss and never find peace. Thieves will steal and never have enough.

> ## Spend a lifetime telling God to be quiet, and he'll do just that.

Hell is not a reform school. There will be no parents to urge you to do the right thing. There will be no preachers to speak about God. God's Spirit won't be there either. Or God's people.

Spend a lifetime telling God to be quiet, and he'll do just that.

Still, God wishes it were different. "I take no pleasure in the death of the wicked, but rather that they turn from their ways and live" (Ezekiel 33:11). Because God is holy, he *must* keep evil from his new universe.

How could a loving God send sinners to hell? He doesn't. They volunteer.

Once there, they don't want to leave. Their hearts never soften. They don't change their minds. What? You don't believe me? Check this out:

> ### HOW COULD a LOVING GOD
> ### SEND SINNERS TO HELL?
> ### He DOESN'T. THEY VOLUNTEER.

"Men were scorched with great heat, and they blasphemed the name of God who has power over these plagues; and they did not repent and give Him glory" (Revelation 16:9 NKJV).

People aren't sorry when they get there. They just have more to be mad about.

Justin, 16

Sometimes my parents' nagging drives me crazy. It seems like they're always mad about something. So I forgot to unload the dishwasher or I didn't study like I should for the test. Big deal. It's not like it's the end of the world or anything.

Sometimes I go along with my parents because I just want them to get off my

> back. That works for some things, but not
> for my salvation. Volunteering to help
> others, following the rules, going to church,
> those are all good things. But that alone
> won't get me through the pearly gates.
> Man, do I realize that now. Accepting
> Jesus, believing in him, and confessing my
> sins is the best choice I ever made.
>
> Faking religion on Sundays won't make a
> difference on the day I die. Hiding Jesus
> the rest of the week won't give me a
> chance to share him with others who need
> him just as much. If I really understood hell,
> how could I let my friends go there with-
> out desperately trying to stop them? It's
> scary to think there are people who don't
> figure these things out till it's too late.

Sometimes hell doesn't seem fair. If God is love, then hell seems to be too harsh. Isn't God overreacting?

A man once accused me of overreacting. Some years ago, when my daughters were small, we came across an annoyed shopper at a store. My three girls were picking doughnuts. They weren't moving quickly enough for him, so he leaned over their shoulders and snapped, "You kids hurry up. You're taking too long."

I was on the next aisle, but I heard and I approached

him. "Sir, those are my daughters. They didn't deserve those words. You need to apologize to them."

He played it down. "I didn't do anything that bad."

I told him I thought he had. Those were my daughters he had hurt. Who was he to challenge my reaction?

Who are we to challenge God's?

Only he knows the full story. He knows the number of invitations the stubborn-hearted have refused. He knows the insults they've spoken.

God isn't unfair.

> TO MAKE IT TO HELL, YOU'D HAVE TO COVER YOUR EARS, BLINDFOLD YOUR EYES, AND IGNORE THE STORY OF JESUS'S SACRIFICE.

He has wrapped caution tape on hell's porch. He's posted a million and one red flags outside the entrance. To make it to hell, you'd have to cover your ears, blindfold your eyes, and ignore the story of Jesus's sacrifice.

If the idea of hell surprises you, this should surprise you more: Christ went to hell so you won't have to. Yet hell could not hold him. He arose not just from the dead but from hell.

Thanks to Christ, this earth can be the nearest you come to hell.

But apart from Christ, this earth is also the nearest you'll come to heaven.

Becca, 17

Okay, my dad calls me a drama queen. Sometimes I overreact about things I think are wrong. Mistakes I think were made. Problems I think should be fixed. Sometimes I'm right, sometimes I'm wrong. But even so, sometimes I overreact and handle it in the wrong way. I can't help it. It's just me. I don't mean to overreact; it's just my first reaction!

I have to admit sometimes I've felt like God was overreacting a little when it came to hell. What about those people who really try to live good lives? Like my next-door neighbor. She had all these chubby Buddha guys all around her house, but she still waved to me whenever I walked by and made me cookies for my birthday. I even heard she gave a kidney to some guy she didn't even know to save his life. Doesn't that mean something?

I suppose no matter how good a person is, it's not good enough. We can't earn our way to heaven. Only God and his son are holy and perfect. What it comes down to is that we have to have faith in his son—that he knows what he's doing. After all, to disagree is to say that I—a human with lots of weaknesses—know more than an all-knowing God! Besides, God offered more than a kidney to save us. And if we don't accept his free gift, then I suppose we have to live with the consequences.

A friend told me about the final hours of her aunt. The woman lived her life with no fear of God or respect for his Word. She was an atheist. Even in her final days, she didn't let anyone speak of God or eternity. Only her Maker knows her last thoughts and eternal destiny. But her family heard her final words. Hours from death, she opened her eyes. No one could see who she talked to, but she spoke these words: "You don't know me? You don't know me?"

Was it Jesus Christ telling her: "I never knew you; depart from me" (Matthew 7:23 ESV)?

Contrast her words with those of a Christ-follower.

The dying man made no secret of his faith. He told

everyone he longed for heaven. Two days before he died from cancer, he awoke from a deep sleep. He told this to his wife: "I'm living in two realities. I'm not allowed to tell you. There are others in this room."

> ## We either face death with fear or faith.

On the day he died, the man opened his eyes and asked, "Am I special? Why, that I should be allowed to see all this?"

We either face death with fear or faith. We either have dread or joy.

God made an offer: "Whoever believes in him shall not perish . . ."

We make the choice.

THINK IT OVER

Sometimes it's easier to think more about the glitter and bling of heaven than the God of heaven. What is one thing you can thank the Hero of heaven for?

....
....
....
....

How would you describe hell? Why do you think God wanted hell to sound so bad?

....
....
....
....

Do you think you will face death with fear or faith? Why?

....
....
....
....

11

What is eternal life?

In one of his *Far Side* cartoons, Gary Larson shows a winged man seated in heaven on a cloud. No one is near. There is nothing to do. He's stuck there. And this is what the caption says: "Wish I'd brought a magazine."[1]

We can relate. *Eternal* life? Clouds, harps, and time on our hands. Forever and ever. Nonstop. An endless sing-along. Hmm . . . that's it?

You might have the same worries. You don't tell anyone, but they're there. Can heaven live up to its promises? Jesus thinks so.

Don't let your hearts be troubled. Trust in God, and trust also in me. There is more than enough room in my Father's home. If this were not so, would I have told you that I am going to prepare a place for you? When everything is ready, I will come and get you, so that you will always be with me where I am. (John 14:1–3 NLT)

The movies have told you wrong. The idea of fog and floating spirits isn't the truth. Forget them. Jesus has gone to "prepare a *place*." Like hell, heaven is touchable.

We guess God will destroy this universe and relocate his children . . . but why would he? When God created the heavens and earth, he applauded his work.

> Can heaven live up to its promises? Jesus thinks so.

God saw:
The light . . . it was good.
The sea . . . it was good.
The grass . . . it was good.
The sun . . . the moon . . . it was good (Genesis 1).
Straight-A report card. "God saw everything that He had made, and indeed it was very good" (Genesis 1:31 NKJV).

But what about the promises of the earth's destruction? Peter and John use A-bomb terminology. "Disappear with a roar . . . destroyed by fire . . . laid bare . . . passed away" (2 Peter 3:10; Revelation 21:1). Won't this planet be destroyed? Yes, but destruction need not mean elimination. Our bodies provide a prototype. They will pass away, return to dust. Yet the one who called Adam out of a dirt pile will do so with us. Christ will reverse decomposition with resurrection. Amino acids will regenerate. Lungs will awaken. Molecules will reconnect. The mortal body will put on immortality (1 Corinthians 15:53).

> **WHEN GOD CREATED THE HEAVENS AND EARTH, HE APPLAUDED HIS WORK.**

The same is true about earth. Paul says that the "whole creation groans and suffers the pains of childbirth together until now" (Romans 8:22 NASB). Like a mother in labor, nature looks toward her delivery day. We see the birth pangs: floods, volcanoes, earthquakes. We contribute to them: polluting the sky, pillaging the soil. God's creation struggles, but not forever. He will purge, cleanse, and reconstruct his cosmos. In the renewal of all things, pristine purity will flow, as Eden promised.

God gives us a peek here of what is to come there. We see gold-drenched sunsets. Diamond-studded night skies. Rainbows that make us stop and sigh. A taste of heaven.

Then there is the New Jerusalem. Christ will come to a city unlike any we've ever seen.

"I, John, saw the holy city, New Jerusalem, coming" (Revelation 21:2 NKJV).

The Bible says it's an exact square of 1,400 miles (Revelation 21:16). That's forty times the size of England, ten times the size of France, and larger than India. And that's just the ground floor!

THERE ARE NO BAD GUYS IN HEAVEN.

The city stands as tall as it does wide. That would be over 600,000 stories, plenty of space for billions of people to come and go.

They will come and go. The gates are never closed (Revelation 21:25). Why shut them? There are no bad guys in heaven. The wicked will be taken care of, leaving only a perfect place of people also made perfect.

In heaven, you will be you at your best forever. Even now you have your good moments. When you're nice to your sibling, forgive your friend's bad mood, and put up with your mom's yelling—you show a little of what you'll be like all the time. Plus, you won't have all the bad stuff about yourself hanging around.

Becca, 17

My Top 10 Things About Heaven

1. I get to see Christ. 1 John 3:2
2. I'll never again be hungry or sad.
   Revelation 7:16-17
3. I'll get a new body! 1 Corinthians 15:50-54;
   2 Corinthians 5:4
4. I'll have a cool room in my Father's house.
   John 14:1-3
5. Great food! Matthew 8:11; Revelation 19:9
6. I get to hang out with Noah, Abraham, Moses,
   Mary, Ruth . . . and more. Hebrews 11-12:1
7. I get to see my Christ-believing family members
   and friends. 1 Thessalonians 4:13-17
8. I won't mess up anymore. I'll be sin free.
   Romans 7:15-25
9. I'll have answers to all my questions.
   1 Corinthians 13:12
10. I'll get a cool, new name! Revelation 2:17

In heaven you will be at your best, and you'll enjoy everyone else at their best too! Won't that be nice?

Even in good families, there are times people are in bad moods. Even on sunny days, people complain. Jesus will make sure there is none of that there. Jesus will suction the last drop of meanness from the deepest parts of our souls.

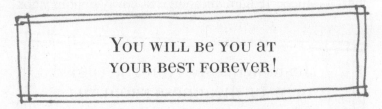

YOU WILL BE YOU AT
YOUR BEST FOREVER!

You'll love the result. No one will doubt your word. Or grade your actions. Or talk about you behind your back.

Dare we imagine heaven's dramatic reunions?

- A soldier embracing the sharpshooter who killed him.
- A daughter seeing her abusive but repentant father and holding him.
- A son encountering the mother who aborted him.

No doubt some will experience such reunions. And when they do, forgiveness will flow like water over Iguaça Falls.

"The wolf will live with the lamb" (Isaiah 11:6). "God will wipe away every tear . . . there shall be no more death, nor sorrow, nor crying . . . for the former things have passed away" (Revelation 21:4 NKJV).

No sin means no thieves, divorce, heartbreak, or boredom. You won't be bored in heaven, because *you* won't be the same you in heaven. Boredom emerges from soils that heaven disallows. The soil of weariness: our eyes tire. Mental limitations: information overload dulls us. Self-centeredness: we grow disinterested when the spotlight shifts to others. Tedium: meaningless activity siphons vigor.

> JESUS WILL SUCTION THE LAST
> DROP OF meanness FROM THE
> DEEPEST PARTS OF OUR SOULS.

All those wrong actions will be in hell with Satan. You will be left with a sharp mind and strong body to follow the jobs God gives you.

Yes, you will have assignments in heaven. (Didn't know that, did you?) God gave Adam and Eve garden responsibilities. He put them in charge over "the fish of the sea, over the birds of the air, and over the cattle, over all the earth and over every creeping thing that creeps on the earth" (Genesis 1:26 NKJV). Adam was placed in the garden "to tend and keep it" (Genesis 2:15 NKJV).

God's people will do it again. "[God's] servants shall serve Him" (Revelation 22:3 NKJV).

What do his happy children do but serve him? Maybe we'll get to do what we do best, only better. Couldn't earthly assignments hint at heavenly ones? Architects might draw blueprints for a new praise arena. We will feast in heaven . . . you may be a cook on Saturn. God filled his first garden with plants and animals. He'll surely do the same in heaven. If so, he may entrust you with the care and feeding of an Africa or two.

> MAYBE WE'LL GET TO DO WHAT
> WE DO BEST, ONLY BETTER.

One thing is for sure: you'll love it.

There will always be more wonderful things about God to discover too. More about his grace. His wisdom. His perfection.

And this is the invitation he gives: "When everything is ready, I will come and get you, so that you will always be with me where I am" (John 14:3 NLT).

Becca, 17

I just really bombed a test. Sometimes I wish I could just graduate and be done with it. I mean, another year of boring lectures, essay questions, and pop quizzes. Not to mention college after that! It's as if adults have it in for their kids or something.

At first, when I heard the idea that we will serve in heaven, I thought, "Oh no, more work." But then, I thought about it. I'll have all the knowledge, strength, and peace I need . . . . no stress! It's not like I'll fail a pop quiz by the pearly gates.

Maybe when I get there I can work in the gardens. I love flowers. I can't even imagine what heavenly flowers will be like.

I love to design clothes too. Maybe I can design new wardrobes for the angels . . . just letting my imagination run wild!

Okay, it's cool. I think I'll love whatever God has me do, because he'll be there and I'll be able to see his smile as I work . . . . and his nod of approval.

No, wait. I changed my mind. I want to be in the choir with all the angels. Then I can praise him all day long. You don't think they make you tryout for a spot, do they?

God, I can't wait for all these amazing things . . .
not to mention the yucky stuff I'll leave behind.

GLIMPSES OF HEAVEN

Circle the good things you've done that give a glimpse of the you in heaven. Cross out the things, attitudes, and sinful desires you can look forward to leaving behind.

- Held the door open for a lady at the grocery store.
- Got down on my knees to seek God's strength.
- Talked back to my mom.
- Helped my friend with his/her homework.
- Thanked God for giving me his Word.
- Took money from my dad's wallet without permission.
- Did something nice for my mom, just because.
- Cursed at a guy I was mad at.
- Lied about my homework assignment being finished, so I could hang out with friends.
- Sang a worship song outside, not caring who heard me.

John Todd was very young when his parents died. He was one of several children, and, as was common in the early 1800s, he and all his siblings were sent to relatives. An aunt offered to take little John. A servant by the name of Caesar was sent to bring John to her. The boy climbed on the back of the horse, wrapped his small arms around the man, and set out for her house. John was scared, but he didn't want to say so. He also had many questions for Caesar.

> ## You are expected.

"Will she be there?"

"Oh, yes," Caesar promised. "She'll be there waiting up for you."

"Will I like living with her?"

"My son, you fall into good hands."

"Will she love me?"

The servant was patient and soft in his reply. "Ah, she has a big heart."

"Do you think she'll go to bed before we get there?"

"Oh, no! She'll be sure to wait up for you. You'll see when we get out of these woods. You'll see her candle in the window."

Sure enough, as they neared the house, John saw a

candle in the window. His aunt was standing in the doorway. As he shyly approached the porch, she reached down and kissed him and said, "Welcome home!"

Young John Todd grew up in his aunt's care. She was a mother to him. When the time came for him to pick a profession, he decided to become a pastor.

Years later, he got news his aunt was dying. Here is what he wrote in reply:

My Dear Aunt,

Years ago, I left a house of death, not knowing where I was to go, whether anyone cared, whether it was the end of me. The ride was long, but the servant encouraged me. Finally I arrived to your embrace and a new home. I was expected; I felt safe. You did it all for me.

Now it's your turn to go. I'm writing to let you know, someone is waiting up, your room is all ready, the light is on, the door is open, and you're expected![2]

You are expected too.

Jesus is preparing a place for you. A perfect place of perfected people. And our perfect Lord is in charge.

And at the right time, he will come and take you home.

Becca, 17

I was with my grandpa when he died. I thought it would be the worst thing ever. Yet he had given his life to Jesus when I was about six or seven, and after that I could tell he loved God. He didn't change and suddenly become a missionary to Africa or something. But I noticed he seemed more content and he didn't use bad words like he used to.

Being with him when he died wasn't scary at all. The day before he died, my grandpa told us he saw Jesus . . . and then he started to cry. They weren't sad tears, they were happy—like he'd just gotten the best gift ever. Then he blew me a kiss . . . like he used to when I was little. And I knew it was going to be all right. He was saying "See you later." And because I have asked Jesus in my heart, I know I will see him. More than that, I'll see Jesus too.

THINK IT OVER

In what ways will the real heaven be different from the cartoons that show fluffy white clouds and angels with harps?

_____
_____
_____
_____

What are you looking forward to most about heaven?

_____
_____
_____
_____

If you could pick one way to serve God in heaven, what would you pick?

_____
_____
_____
_____

12

What difference does salvation make?

> **3:16—". . . shall not perish
> but have eternal *life*"**

A friend from my West Texas hometown contacted me with some big news. "My father saw your mother's name in an unclaimed property column of the local newspaper."

I couldn't imagine what the property might be. Dad died years ago. Mom lives near my sister in Arkansas. We sold her house. As far as I knew, we owned nothing in the city. "Unclaimed property?"

"Sure, city hall is required to list the names of folks who own these goods."

"You don't say."

"I'll send you the contact information."

That was on Sunday. His e-mail arrived on Tuesday. That left me the better part of forty-eight hours to imagine what my folks, unknown to their kids, had hid away. At first I was puzzled. The Great Depression turned my parents into penny-pinchers. They did to dollars what boa constrictors do to rats—squeezed the life out of them.

> MY IMAGINATION RACED LIKE A RACE CAR DRIVER. THIS COULD BE BIG.

Then again, Dad worked as an oil-field mechanic. Did someone convince him to quietly invest a few bucks in an oil well? Did he keep it from Mom so she wouldn't erupt?

And now, could it be that the oil well has hit the big one? A gusher might mean millions, no zillions of barrels of black gold. And who is listed among the investors but Jack Lucado. And who is listed among his heirs?

My imagination raced like a race car driver. *This could be big.*

By Sunday evening I imagined enough money for my yet-to-be-born grandchildren's education. On Monday I ended world hunger. Tuesday, as the e-mail came, I was solving the AIDS crisis.

I dialed the courthouse number. The clerk remembered my mom. She was excited. "I've been hoping you'd call." I heard papers shuffling. "Now where did I put that check?" she mumbled.

Check? Gulp. I pulled a calculator out of my desk and flexed my fingers.

"Here it is!" she exclaimed, speaking back into the phone. "Looks like we owe your mom some money. Whoa, this has been here for a while."

I drummed my fingers on the desk.

"Let's see, Mister Lucado. Where should we send this check?"

I gave her an address and waited.

She continued. "Looks like we owe your mom three fifty."

Did she say th-th-three hundred and fifty million? I collected myself. She might mean thousand. Whichever, way to go, Dad.

> SOME HOPES FAIL TO DELIVER.
> SOME EXPECTATIONS DEFLATE
> LIKE AN UNTIED BALLOON.

"Yes, sir, your mother overpaid her final water bill by three dollars and fifty cents. Shall I send that today?"

"Sure . . . thanks. Just put it in the mail."

Some hopes fail to deliver. Some expectations deflate like an untied balloon.

Becca, 17

With all this talk of eternity and life, I've been thinking more about the future lately. I thought I'd start by focusing on my most important hopes, dreams, and goals. I'm going to ask my friends to fill them in too. What do you think?

If I knew I only had ten years to live, I would:

1. Finish high school and college.
2. Find a great person to marry.
3. Lead others to Jesus.
4. Go on a missionary trip to tell others about Jesus.
5. Spend time with my friends.
6. Travel Europe.
7. Find my dream job.
8. Read the Bible all the way through.
9. Write a movie script . . . and see it come to life on the big screen.
10. Go on an African safari with my family.

If I knew I only had six months to live, I would:

1. *Spend time with my friends and family.*
2. *Read the Bible all the way through.*
3. *Pray more.*
4. *Go on a missionary trip to tell others about Jesus.*
5. *Take a road trip with my friends.*

What if I only had one day?

1. *All I need is Jesus.*

"If only" dreams are different for each person. "If only I made the team . . . could have my own car . . . got asked out on a real date." The only wall between you and happiness is an "if only."

THE ONLY WALL BETWEEN YOU AND HAPPINESS IS AN "IF ONLY."

Then it happens. You make the team, get the car, and go on the date . . . but it's not what you expected.

Life has letdowns. And how do you know Christ won't be one of them? Honestly.

He has big promises. Life. Eternal life. "Whoever believes in him shall not perish but have eternal life" (John 3:16). If we were on the 3:16 road trip, with this chapter we'd be pulling into the final destination. There is just one more word to think about: *life.*

Life in this verse doesn't mean the length of life on earth but eternal life. Jesus offers more—something a jersey, a car, or a date can never do. And you'll love how he does it. Jesus reconnects your soul with God.

What God gave Adam and Eve, he also gave to you and me. A soul.

> ## JESUS RECONNECTS YOUR SOUL WITH GOD.

Read this: "The LORD God formed man of the dust of the ground, and breathed into his nostrils the breath of life; and man became a living being" (Genesis 2:7 NKJV).

You, a grandchild of an ape? A chemical fluke? An atomic surprise? By no means. You hold inside you the very breath of God. He exhaled himself into you, and you became a "living being" (Genesis 2:7).

Your soul distinguishes you from zoo dwellers. God

gifted the camel with a hump and the giraffe with a flag-pole neck, but he reserved his breath, or a soul, for you. You bear his stamp. You do things God does. Think. Question. Reflect. You blueprint buildings, chart sea crossings, and feel your heart warm when you hug your grandma. You, like Adam, have a soul.

> YOU HOLD INSIDE YOU THE
> VERY BREATH OF GOD.

And, like Adam, you've used your soul to disobey God. God's command to the first couple is also the first time death is mentioned: "You must not eat from the tree of the knowledge of good and evil, for when you eat of it you will surely die" (Genesis 2:17).

Sin resulted in Adam's and Eve's immediate deaths. But death of what? Their bodies? No, they continued to breathe. Brain waves flowed. Eyelids blinked. Their bodies functioned, but their hearts hardened. They stopped trusting God. Their friendship with their maker died.

Deep within we've known (haven't we?) something is awry—we feel disconnected. What we hope will bring life brings limited amounts . . . three fifty's worth. We have fun with friends, find meaning in family, yet long for something more.

Justin, 16

I've heard it said that when God seems far away, he isn't the one that moved. It's not like I moved—or meant to if I did. Stalled would be a better word. Like a car that sputters as it gets close to running out of gas.

I read my Bible, but I forget what I read as soon as I close it. And prayer . . . well, sometimes it's hard to talk when no one is talking back. Then I got the idea of picturing "Jesus" in the faces around me. After all, didn't Jesus say when I take care of "the least of these," I'm doing it for him?

It may sound crazy, but when I mow the lawn for my mom, I picture myself doing it for Jesus. The same with the extra laps my coach tells me to do. The burn doesn't seem so bad when I imagine running for God.

Somehow, when I live out my salvation this way, it helps me respect others and respect God. Go figure. It's another thing that really works, if we just try it God's way.

When we long for something more, sometimes we feel the frustration I felt on Christmas morning, 1964. I assembled a nine-year-old's dream gift: a genuine Santa Fe Railroad miniature train set, complete with battery-powered engine and flashing crossing lights. I placed the locomotive on the tracks and watched in sheer glee as three pounds of pure steel wound its way across my bedroom floor. Around and around and around and . . . around . . . and around . . . After some time I picked it up and turned it the other direction. It went around and around and around . . .

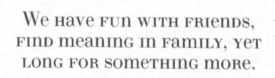

We HAVE FUN WITH FRIENDS,
FIND MEANING IN FAMILY, YET
LONG FOR SOMETHING MORE.

"Mom, what else did you get me for Christmas?"

Just like that, our lives chug in long ovals, one lap after another. Around and around . . . Is there anything else?

Thankfully, Jesus gives us a way to reconnect.

He breathes life into flatlined lives. He does for our hearts what we do for dead car batteries.

"Because Jesus was raised from the dead, we've been given a brand-new life and have everything to live for, including a future in heaven—and the future starts now!" (1 Peter 1:3–4 MSG).

Others offer life, but no one offers to do what Jesus does—to reconnect us to his power. But how can we know? How do we know that Jesus knows what he's talking about? The best answer, according to his first followers, is the empty tomb.

> **BUT HOW can we know? How do we know that Jesus knows what he's talking about?**

Did you catch how amazing that is? "Because Jesus was *raised from the dead,* we've been given a brand-new life."

Can Jesus actually replace death with life? He did a good job with his own. We can trust him because he has been there.

He's been there . . .

He's been to Bethlehem, wearing barn rags and hearing sheep eat. God himself found inside an eight-pound body and happy to sleep on a cow's supper. Millions who face empty pockets or other fears of life turn to Christ. Why?

Why seek Jesus's help with your challenges? Because he's been there. To Nazareth, to Galilee, to Jerusalem.

But most of all, he's been to the grave. Not as a visitor, but as a dead body. Heart silent and lungs empty. The cemetery. He's been buried there.

You haven't yet. But you will be. And since you will, don't you need someone who knows the way out?

> God . . . has given us new birth into a living hope through the resurrection of Jesus Christ from the dead. . . . He destroyed death, and through the Good News he showed us the way to have life that cannot be destroyed. (1 Peter 1:3 NIV; 2 Timothy 1:10 NCV)

Remember that check from my hometown? I'm still waiting on it. Not counting on it for much. The three fifty promises to bring little. But the 3:16 promise? I've long since deposited that check. It bears interest every day and will forever.

Yours will too.

Justin, 16

Sometimes I head out expecting an adventure—like when I was a kid and my Boy Scout troop went on a week-long camp out . . . miles from the rest of the world. Other times adventure seems to find me. I feel that way with 3:16. Yet instead of a hike out into the woods, it's been a trip deep inside. Places I never knew existed . . .

which is a totally weird thought. Whole places inside. Soul places.

I feel I understand God better—his sacrifice, his love, and how much my choices make or break what he wants to do with my life. Still, there are areas I think . . . no wait, I know . . . I haven't conquered yet. Like wasting time on video games and other completely unimportant things. Or attitudes toward people that still tick me off—no matter how much I try to love them. Or prejudices against people or groups of people I don't even know.

God, it's been a hike, and I know we're not through. In fact, WE won't be until I see you face-to-face. But until that time, will you do me a favor? Will you grow bigger in my view? And can you knock me on the side of the head when I'm not quite getting it—with as much love as you have in you, of course. Finally, will you give me a heart that wants to do what matters most? A heart like yours. Yeah, I think that's everything. Thanks.

THINK IT OVER

Sometimes we thank God for our future salvation. In what ways does his gift of salvation help you today?

_____

_____

_____

_____

What would you have done differently today if you would have "seen Jesus" in the faces around you?

_____

_____

_____

_____

What challenges are you asking Jesus to help you with?

_____

_____

_____

_____

my notes

_____
_____
_____
_____
_____
_____
_____
_____
_____
_____
_____
_____
_____
_____
_____
_____
_____
_____

My Notes

My Notes

endnotes

CHAPTER 2

1. Andy Christofides, *The Life Sentence: John 3:16* (Waynesboro, GA: Paternoster Publishing, 2002), 11.
2. Guillermo Gonzalez and Jay W. Richards, *The Privileged Planet: How Our Place in the Cosmos Is Designed for Discovery* (Washington, DC: Regnery Publishing, 2004), 143.
3. Christofides, *The Life Sentence*, 13.
4. "Liftoff to Space Exploration," NASA, http://liftoff.msfc.nasa.gov/academy/universe_travel.html.
5. Bob Sheehan, "A Self-Revealing God," *Reformation Today*, no. 127, May–June 1992, 6.
6. Bill Tucker (speech, Oak Hills Church men's conference, San Antonio, TX, May 3, 2003).

CHAPTER 4

1. Ker Than, "Pluto Is Now Just a Number: 134340," MSNBC.com, http://msnbc.msn.com/id/14789691.
2. John S. Feinberg, gen. ed., *No One Like Him: The Doctrine of God* (Wheaton, IL: Crossway Books, 2001), 349.
3. R. Laird Harris, Gleason Archer, and Bruce K. Waltke, eds. *Theological Wordbook of the Old Testament*, vol. 1 (Chicago: Moody, 1980), 332, quoted in Feinberg, *No One Like Him*, 349.
4. W. E. Vine, *Expository Dictionary of New Testament Words: A Comprehensive Dictionary of the Original Greek Words with Their Precise Meanings for English Readers* (McClean: VA: MacDonald Publishing Company, n.d.), 703.

CHAPTER 5

1. Edward W. Goodrick, ed., John R. Kohlenberger III and James A. Swann, assoc. eds., *Zondervan NIV Exhaustive Concordance*, 2nd ed. (Grand Rapids, MI: Zondervan Publishing House, 1999), 4778, #4742.

CHAPTER 6

1. *Heaven and Home Hour Radio Bulletin*, http://www.sermonillustrations.com/ a-z/s/sinful_nature.htm (accessed August 4, 2007).
2. Stanley Barnes, comp., *Sermons on John 3:16* (Greenville, SC: AmbassadorProductions, 1999), 79.
3. Alan Cohen, *Paco, Come Home, A 3rd Serving of Chicken Soup for the Soul: 101 More Stories to Open the Heart and Rekindle the Spirit*, compiled by Jack Canfield and Mark Victor Hansen (Deerfield Beach, FL: Health Communications, Inc., 1996), 78.

CHAPTER 7

1. Francis William Boreham, *A Handful of Stars*, quoted in Barnes, comp., *Sermons on John 3:16* (Greenville, SC: Ambassador Productions, 1999), 19–20. The wording of the verse probably followed the most popular English translation of the day, the King James Version: "For God so loved the world, that he gave his only begotten Son, that whosoever believeth in him should not perish, but have everlasting life."
2. Larry Dixon, *The Other Side of the Good News* (Wheaton, IL: Victor Books, 1992), 133.

CHAPTER 9

1. David Tereshchuk, "Racing Towards Inclusion," Team Hoyt, http://www.teamhoyt.com/history.shtml.
2. R. C. Zaehner, ed., *Encyclopedia of World Religions* (New York: Barnes & Noble, 1997), s.v. "Hinduism."

3. Dan McKinley, "Aren't All Religions Just Different Ways to the Same Place?" The Coaching Center, http://www.gocampus.org/modx/ index.php?id=109.
4. John Blanchard, *Whatever Happened to Hell?* (Wheaton, IL: Crossway Books, 1995), 62.
5. Dave Hunt, *Whatever Happened to Heaven?* (Eugene, OR: Harvest House Publishers, 1988), 14, quoted in Blanchard, *Whatever Happened to Hell?*, 62.
6. Peter Cotterell, *London Bible College Review*, Summer 1989, quoted in Peter Lewis, *The Glory of Christ* (London: Hodder and Stoughton, 1992), 461.

CHAPTER 10
1. 1 Corinthians 1:18.
2. Robert Jeffress, *Hell? Yes! . . . and Other Outrageous Truths You Can Still Believe* (Colorado Springs, CO: WaterBrook Press, 2004), 73.
3. Blanchard, *Whatever Happened to Hell?*, 105.

CHAPTER 11
1. Randy Alcorn, *Heaven* (Wheaton, IL: Tyndale House Publishers, 2004), 6–7.
2. Robert Strand, *Moments for Mothers* (Green Forest, AR: New Leaf Press, 1996), excerpted in Jack Canfield and others, *A 4th Course of Chicken Soup for the Soul: 101 More Stories to Open the Heart and Rekindle the Spirit* (Deerfield Beach, FL: Health Communications, 1997), 200–01.